WRITING RE:WRITING SERIES

PROSES

Carolyn Kizer

Carolyn Kizer

PROSES

On Poems & Poets

COPPER CANYON PRESS

"The Stories of My Life" was printed in the Contemporary Authors Series, published by Gale Research.

The pieces on Emily Dickinson and Louise Bogan first appeared in the *San Jose Mercury News;* the editor of its book section also took the extraordinary step of devoting an entire issue to the essay on Maynard Mack's biography of Alexander Pope; the coda, on Pope and poets, was a lecture given at Centrum in Port Townsend.

"The Green Man" is greatly expanded from the introduction to *The Essential John Clare* (Ecco Press, 1992).

"A Note on Robinson Jeffers" appeared in a special issue of *Quarry West* devoted to that poet.

"The Poetics of Water" was first given as a Lenten Sermon at the Cathedral of St. John the Divine, New York, and was subsequently printed in the *Denver Quarterly.*

"So Big" appeared in *Open Places.*

The reviews of the following appeared in the *New York Times Book Review* in somewhat different form: John Berryman, Carol Muske, Laura Jensen, John Ash, Robert Hass, James Merrill, and Don Pagis.

The reviews of a volume of Karl Shapiro's autobiography and Gary Snyder's poems appeared in the *Los Angeles Times Book Review.*

"Others Call it God" appeared in an issue of the *Seneca Review* devoted to the work of Hayden Carruth.

"Wrapped in Silk: Marie Ponsot" was printed by *Poetry Flash.*

The review of the Sylvia Plath biography appeared in *U.S.A. Today.*

"Growing Old Alive: Kenneth Hanson and Han Yü" appeared in *Willow Springs.*

The *Washington Post Book World* printed the reviews of poets Robert Creeley, Carolyn Forché, Josephine Jacobsen, Denise Levertov, Marge Piercy, Adrienne Rich, Lorine Niedecker, Edward Hirsch, Linda Gregg, C.K. Williams, and Frank Bidart.

Publication of this book is supported by a grant from the National Endowment for the Arts and a grant from the Lannan Foundation. Additional support to Copper Canyon Press has been provided by the Andrew W. Mellon Foundation, the Lila Wallace-Reader's Digest Fund, and the Washington State Arts Commission. Copper Canyon Press is in residence with Centrum at Fort Worden State Park.

Library of Congress Cataloging-in-Publication Data
Kizer, Carolyn.
Proses : on poems & poets / Carolyn Kizer.
p.   cm.
ISBN, 1-55659-045-8 : $12.00
1. Kizer, Carolyn—Biography. 2. Poets, American—20th century—
Biography. 3. Poetics. 4. Poetry. I. Title.
PS3521.I9Z474   1993
811'.54—dc20
[b]   93-31586
CIP

COPPER CANYON PRESS
P.O. Box 271, Port Townsend, Washington 98368

TABLE OF CONTENTS

———————

An Exaltation of Poets

TO
DIANE JOHNSON
&
URSULA LEGUIN

PROSES

The Stories of My Life

THE FIRST KIZER—or Keyser as it was then spelt—to leave the home of his ancestors in Holland was the Reverend Dirck Keyser, son of Gerrits Keyser, a silk merchant in Amsterdam. He came to Germantown, Pennsylvania, as a Dutch Mennonite preacher in 1690, bringing his wife and three children," wrote my father in a memoir which he has left to me. "Dirck Keyser's sons took to farming, down in the Shenandoah Valley in Virginia, west of where the city of Washington was to be built a hundred years later.

"There, succeeding generations changed the Dutch 'Keyser' to 'Kizer,' and dropped names such as Dirck and Gerrits for English Bible names such as John, Simon, and Joseph. There they farmed the land and raised large families. In 1809, my great-grandfather Joseph Kizer...made a horseback journey into western Ohio, and there he selected 160 acres in the deep woods of what was later Champaign County, where his descendants still farm the land." After obtaining a patent signed by President Jefferson, he moved his wife and two little children and their household goods to Ohio, then a journey of six weeks. "There, within a year, their third child, my grandfather Benjamin, was born to them." His son was Frank Kizer, who married Mary Hamilton, Scots daughter of a Springfield physician whose family, like the Kizers, came from Virginia. A year later, in 1878, my father was born.

My grandparents settled on a farm which had been given them by my great-grandfather as a wedding gift. Grandfather had not wanted to be a farmer, but he had only had a year at Oberlin College, and now his father insisted that he settle down. He stood it for four years, and then managed to sell the farm back to his stern, disapproving father, and set up as a small-town merchant. Farm life hadn't agreed with my father either. He was subject to severe hay fever and must have been allergic to practically everything on the farm. And he hated farm food: the enormous platters heaped with meat and potatoes and liberally slathered with gravy to satisfy the farmhand's appetites nauseated him. (At home we rarely had meat, we never had mashed potatoes, and never gravy.)

Father's first memory was of the farm, when he couldn't have been older than three:

One day I climbed into the pigpen to see the new litter of baby pigs, and the mother pig bit me," Father said. "So I kicked the pig. Just then my father came around the corner of the barn and saw me. And because I had kicked the pig he gave me a whipping. I felt the terrible injustice of this, and decided to run away from home. I didn't get very far, as my legs were short, and I soon settled down behind a haystack in the near field. Pretty soon my mother came to the back door and began calling to me, 'Ben! Ben! Come to supper now!' I'm sure I had been in that field all of fifteen minutes and I was dying of hunger, but nothing would induce me to speak. 'Ben! Ben!' Mother kept calling, 'Where are you, Ben?' I could bear it no longer. 'I won't anxer!' I cried.

Like Father's people, Mother's, both the Ashleys and the Warrens, came from Virginia; but they were of English stock. My grandfather William Washington Ashley was a descendant of the first Earl of Shaftesbury, Anthony Ashley Cooper, and of the elder brother of George Washington. My grandmother Carolyn Warren descended from one Martin Warren, who fought in the Revolution, after which he settled in Missouri, founded the town of Warrensberg, and spent the rest of his life as a blacksmith. (Thanks to Martin Warren, Mother was able to join the Daughters of the American Revolution at the time they barred the great singer Marian Anderson from their hall in Washington, D.C., solely because she was black. Mother joined so that she could raise some serious hell about this outrage, a quite characteristic act compounded of fury and glee.)

Grandfather Ashley was orphaned as an infant, and one of my mother's stories which made a great impression on me was of how her great-aunt Eliza, who was engaged to a Union captain, Richard Merriweather Box, used to drive a buggy through the Southern and Union lines during the Civil War, with the baby beside her on the seat, to visit her fiancé.

Carolyn Warren, for whom I am named, was a beauty, with black hair, dead white skin, and violet eyes. "She despised her nickname," my mother told me. "'Care-worn!' she would cry, in her soft Southern accent, 'I'm *not* care-worn!'" (I wonder if my aversion to nicknames stems from hers. I coped with this as a child by simply refusing to answer if addressed by anything other than my full name.) Like my Kizer grandmother, she was a year or two older than Grandfather, and self-conscious about it. She was an ardent Democrat, and he, like most doctors, a staunch Republican. "He called her 'mouse-ears,'" Mother said, "and she called him 'donkey-ears.'" Grandfather graduated in the first class of Belleview, Mother told me, and shortly after he began to practice medicine they moved to the Colorado mountains because both of them had tuberculosis. There, my mother and her brothers were born, one right after another. Poor Grandmother! By the time of her early death, right after my youngest uncle was born, she must have been careworn indeed.

In St. Paris, from 1881 to 1890, my father spent the hardest, most toilsome years of his life," my father wrote, "in a desperate attempt to make a go of an enterprise that was doomed from the start." For one thing, he had stocked fine china, which was his special pride, but no one would buy it. "Farms, not china were the hobby of those who had money. Bit by bit, the noose grew tighter. Finally, when my father was thirty-three, he could go on no longer. He was forced to turn everything over to his creditors." His humiliation over this disgrace marked him for the rest of his life. "To him it seemed important that the Kizers, whom he thought of as the oldest and best family in the region, had never had a failure among them. Father had secretly thought himself smarter than the others, sure to carry the credit of the family to greater heights." The only thing to do was to move far, far away. So Grandfather headed west, and stopped at the little town of Spokane, in Eastern Washington.

"Ouray, the little town where we grew up, was high in the Colorado

Mountains—12,000 feet," Mother said. (It was more like 7,800, but Mother had a highly developed dramatic sense, and twelve sounded better.) "It never occurred to us that skis were for recreation; we used them to get around on most of the year. And sledding too—although sometimes we sledded for fun. One Sunday when we should have been in church, the five little Ashleys dragged their sled way up the side of the mountain, and we slid all the way into town; the doors of the Episcopal church were wide open, and the service was going on, the choir was singing, as the sled shot down the center aisle and bumped up against the altar!" (I visited that little church last summer; the door faces away from the mountain and it would have been impossible to enter in that fashion.)

Grandfather Kizer's first job in Spokane was as a clerk in a grocery store. But soon he became bookkeeper and office manager for a wholesale butter-and-egg distributor. He was an attractive man who made friends easily, in his church and in the Republican party. In less than three years after arriving in Spokane, he became one of three city commissioners. I have a wonderful photograph of Grandfather as fire commissioner, presiding in civilian clothes over his firemen, who look as funny as Keystone Cops. Because he was a public official, my grandfather managed to escape the calamitous results of the panic of 1893; but Frank Kizer had dreamed of returning to St. Paris, Ohio, in triumph, a successful man in a frock coat and a silk hat, to obliterate forever the memory of his disgrace. Every effort by every family member was bent towards this goal; the little boys worked at odd jobs; my grandmother, after her normal thirteen-hour day, baked bread at night for the boys to peddle the next day. But only a year after the panic Spokane was in the midst of a wild mining boom. Speculators poured into town; new mining companies were quickly organized, and wiser heads than Grandfather's plunged into dubious investments. Finally, Grandfather couldn't resist: he resigned as city commissioner, and bought into a mine called The Lily May. He lost everything, including the top hat and the new frock coat.

"Your grandfather was the doctor for the towns of Montrose and Telluride as well as Ouray," Mother told me. "Those were terrible times. If a miner was injured in an accident, the company just fired him. No workman's compensation or insurance or anything like that. His family was lucky not to starve. And when the miners tried to strike, the company would lock them into boxcars and shunt the train from Ouray to Montrose to Telluride and back again. The women would run down to the tracks and try to throw them food and bottles of water. The men were just packed into those cars like the Jews under Hitler." And when the miners were hurt, my grandfather tried to patch them up, most of the time without being paid anything. All this made a lifelong radical out of Mother.

The second ruin of Grandfather Kizer was, as my father put it, the last blow. "When he was only forty, my father suffered a stroke. Instead of the handsome, affable, magnetic man I had always known, my father was an invalid, bewildered, deeply self-critical, pathetically dependent on the rest of us." (A characteristic of both my grandfathers was that they were rotten businessmen. Whatever they touched turned to dross, the difference being that Grandfather Ashley was a successful doctor and brilliant diagnostician. God knows what my poor grandfather Kizer should have been! At any rate, I inherited their impracticality; the women in my family were the shrewd and provident ones.)

Shortly after that, Grandfather, who was also growing deaf, was walking on the trestle bridge over Hangman's Creek where supposedly he failed to hear the train coming behind him. He was instantly killed. (Of course one wonders about suicide, although it seemed clear that this supposition had not occurred to his son.) My father had to drop out of school to become the sole support of the family, which included a younger brother and sister. In addition to selling newspapers on the streets of Spokane he went to work as a bookkeeper in a hardware store (and when he left, he was succeeded by a lad named Henry J. Kaiser, for whom my father was general counsel when Kaiser was building Grand Coulee Dam—leading, obviously, to endless confusion).

"The next three-and-a-half years were the bitterest of my life," my father wrote. "The one thing I wanted above everything else was an education. I was deeply rebellious, not against my father, but against the fate that had involved me in his second ruin. I could see no escape."

"This is a picture of the most beautiful girl in Ouray," Mother said. "The whole family lived in a two-room house. Her little brother was an idiot who was kept chained to a bedstead in the front room." He babbled and drooled, and had no control over his bodily functions. "She could never bring friends home because of her brother. All the boys were in love with her, but she wouldn't see any of them. As they both grew older, she became more and more desperate, and finally she ran away and went on the streets. There was nothing else for her to do."

In addition to working a seventy-hour week at McGowan Brothers hardware store, my father found additional employment reading aloud to an Episcopal clergyman and to a few elderly lawyers and judges who had fled the South in the days of Reconstruction. They were the town's intellectuals, men of large learning and extensive libraries. "This nourished my love of books," Father said. "No one else had these beautiful volumes, row on row, covered in red leather with the names stamped in gold on their spines! So I determined to become a lawyer, so that I could have such a library for my own."

My mother and her two brothers, Rob and Charles, often spoke of my grandfather Ashley as a stern disciplinarian. One day when Rob and Ray, the two oldest boys, were still very young they met the owner of the livery stable and chorused, "Hello, Sam!" My grandfather happened to overhear them, and instantly dragged the boys off to the woodshed for a severe whipping. "Never again do I want to hear you call a grown man by his first name!" The boys protested that they didn't know that Sam had a last name, to no avail. Forty years later, they were still bitter about this. But to the granddaughter who visited him and her uncles in California, Grandfather was soft and indulgent. I still remember from the age of six or so when I had been begging for more candy, Grandfather saying, "Oh, let the baby have what she wants!" and the long long look which my mother and my uncle Rob exchanged. I can't help but believe that the lifelong insecurities of that handsome and gifted generation grew in part from the harshness and severity of my grandfather's discipline. On the other side, I think that my father's enormous self-confidence developed under the aegis of a gentle father and an adoring mother.

With less than two years of high school and none of college, Father determined to enter the Law School of the University of Michigan, which in those days you could do without having an undergraduate degree. "I camped in the office of the President until he would see me," Father said. "He just laughed at me and turned me down. So I went back every morning at eight o'clock and sat in his office, till finally I wore him out, and he admitted me. 'Now I hope I've seen the last of you,' he said. 'Well, no,' I told him. 'Now I want you to admit my brother Don.' He just threw up his hands, but eventually he let Don in as well."

"When I was seventeen," Mother said, "I was chosen to ride on the float in the annual parade. I already had a white organdy dress for church, but Mother made me the most beautiful sash I had ever seen: turquoise blue silk with a long bow in the back. When I rode on the float I was so proud! I waved at the crowd standing along the street, and dropped my new embroidered handkerchief. A rough-looking miner picked it up and put it in his pocket." The next day, she went with her father to the mine, where one of the miners had had an accident. At the mine entrance stood the man who had picked up her handkerchief, and fixing her "with a lewd grin," he masturbated into it. "So I went home and took my beautiful blue sash that I loved so much and I opened the door of the stove and pushed it in and burnt it up."

Father had a desperate time at college. Having saved every penny while he was working in Spokane to keep his mother going, he now took on a variety of jobs to support himself, including digging ditches and writing theses for the other, lazier men. I have in my possession his little account book, where a typical entry is, "Collar turned: one penny." I always weep when I read it. He was tall, thin, undernourished, and frail. Inevitably, the life of unceasing labor and study caught up with him. His whole system rebelled: what food he ate he vomited up, and he went blind. A fellow student from Spokane, Ed Powell, nursed him and read case notes aloud to him in these, his darkest hours. This forged a friendship that lasted all their long lives as practicing attorneys in Spokane. After a rest of several months that winter, he regained his sight. "And the doctor told me never to take stimulants – coffee, tea – to go easy on meat, which I didn't care for anyway, not to smoke and never to drink. And get plenty of exercise." He took this advice and lived by it for the rest of his life. He walked, hiked, climbed. Well into middle age, he could still walk forty miles. As soon as he returned to Spokane, he began to carry a cane, for pleasure. And I suspect he thought it made him look more mature. He carried it all his life; it was his totem, his hallmark: swinging his cane as he strode along Second Street on his way to the office. If by any chance he mislaid it, strangers would come up to him in the street, saying, "Mr. Kizer, where is your cane?"

When Mother was thirteen her own mother died. This was a wound to my mother that never healed – and which was passed on to me. "When my mother died, I never forgave myself for being impudent and disobedient. If anything should happen to me, I wouldn't want you to have that burden of guilt." The message was, of course, "Be good, or else!" When Rollin, her favorite brother, sustained an injury on the football field, he became paralyzed for life, which was a decade until he was twenty-six. He became the family saint: winsome, spiritual, beautiful. And, like all the Ashleys, he was endowed with – or developed, lying helpless day after tedious day – extraordinary intuitions, perceptions, ESP, call it what you will. "Charles [Mother's youngest brother], almost as soon as he could walk, looked after Rollin: washed him, fed him, turned him over in bed. Later, Charles might be on the dance floor miles away, and he would drop the girl right in the middle of the floor and run out, saying, 'Rollin wants me.'" And Rollin did.

One night, my grandfather, who had gone up the mountain to deliver a baby, didn't return and didn't return, and everyone was worried. "'It was a breech birth, and twins, and the horse has gone lame. Dad will be home about five in the morning. He's dead tired,' Rollin said." And so it was. Grandfather staggered in, heaving off his muddy coat, and telling them about it, word for word, at five in the morning.

My father graduated from Michigan Law School, Phi Beta Kappa, in 1902, was admitted to the Michigan Bar, and returned to Spokane to practice law for the rest of his life. Meanwhile Mother was going to the University of Colorado, in Boulder, to get her degree in biology. The last time I looked, she was still on the walls of the Pi Phi House in Boulder, in a group picture, the very model of a glorious Gibson Girl. Then Grandfather, who had remarried and started a second family, moved the whole tribe to California. Mother went on to get her advanced degree in biology at Stanford, in 1904.

Mother had wonderful stories about teaching kindergarten in San Francisco for Chinese tots, and running a summer camp for impoverished children near Muir Woods. My favorite San Francisco story concerns a time when the Powell Street cable snapped, and the cable car slid all the way down the steep hill, to crash into a waiting truck at Union Square. An ancient Chinese inquired of Mother, "Whatsa molla? Stling bloke?" But for the most part, their stories of childhood and growing up had ceased, to be replaced by fragmentary memories called up at odd moments. There was something like a twenty-year hiatus until they met each other, and the family romance began.

Father proposed to Mother on a sofa on the balcony of the famed Davenport Hotel, two weeks after they had met, he then being a widower in his later forties, Mother a spinster in her early forties. This bench was a shrine of my youth, often revisited. Father jokingly suggested to Mr. Davenport that he be permitted to buy the sofa; sometime in the sixties it disappeared.

I came along not too long after their marriage, conceived, I was told, on March 12, at Lake Louise, in Canada. On the night I was born, December 10, my father went for a long walk under the stars while my mother was in labor, and then went home and wrote me a letter, to be delivered on my eighteenth birthday.

Your mother had just been taken to the delivery room, where she was given over to the care of doctors and nurses among whom she was to endure the travail of your birth, while your father was sent out into the night. . . . There was no moon nor a cloud in the sky, and in the crisp, sparkling air, the stars were at their nearest to earth. Sirius was there, high in the south; Capella was there, low in the northwest, near to her setting; Vega was there, just risen in the northeast; and well up in the east was Arcturus. The four brightest, most beautiful of all our stars, so rarely to be seen together, were shining down upon your birth. . . . It is at just such poignant moments as these that the voices of the Universe become articulate to us. It is when our spirits are stabbed broad awake that we can listen, that we can feel the everlasting arms of the God at the heart of all being. Why do I tell you this? You too will suffer pain, emotion too keen for the human breast to bear alone. When it comes, when it seems unbearable, walk out-of-doors if you can. There will be the

wind of the dawn, or the sun of noonday, or the stars of night. There
will be the pine trees and the hills, or perhaps the sweet rain. . . .

I believe that this is the closest my father ever came to poetry. He
lived so energetically in the world that I am afraid that I came to feel
that Mother was in sole charge of the poetic, artistic part of my life —
this despite the fact that he read aloud to us every night of our lives
when we were at home, beginning when I was five or so. If you should
be mad enough to want your child to grow up to be a writer, I can
guarantee this method, doubled in my case because Mother read aloud
to me too.

Me. I. Who was I? I found a slip of paper in the book of my early life
which my mother so scrupulously kept. It reads, in part, "Eleanor Ashley Kizer, Isabel Ashley Kizer, Evelyn Ashley Kizer, Sylvia Ashley
Kizer, Janet Ashley Kizer," and finally, "Carolyn Ashley Kizer." And
by each name are a number of initials; evidently Mother's friends voted
on the names! I am glad that "Carolyn" won. I am one of those rare
people who has always been fond of her name. However, it has occurred to me that bits of Eleanor (queenly, imperious), Isabel (the
cold selfish villainess), Evelyn (wishy-washy old Evelyn), Sylvia (un-
predictable wood-nymph), and Janet (reliable horse) were digested by
my psyche as well. From childhood through adolescence when I would
come down to breakfast, Mother frequently inquired, in tones of irony,
"And who are we this morning?"

It may be another sign of my shaky sense of identity that I had not
one imaginary playmate but four: Ling, Ding, Kootoo, and Grease, or
Greece. Ling was the dominant one (and where I got those Chinese
names I have no idea), a boy, as were Ding and Kootoo (who, it is
conceivable, was Japanese); Greece was a girl who lived in the water
tower across the river that I could see from my bedroom window. I believe that the boys were in residence. I remember shouting at our
phlegmatic, literal-minded laundress, Mrs. Anderson, "Get up! Get up!
You are sitting on Ling!" I can still see the look of somewhat bovine
bewilderment on her good face as she rose heavily and looked behind
her at an empty chair.

I have often been asked how I managed not to be crushed by two strong, articulate, and dominating parents. Long ago I found a formula for replying to such queries: "Inside this body of a road-company Valkyrie is a small, bedraggled brown sparrow." Like all such formulae, it is a lie with a kernel of truth. One way of handling my family situation was by parroting the opinions of my parents. We were an intensely political family, and as I was one of those repellent children who was allowed to dine with the grown-ups, I felt free to express opinions on the news of the day about which I was only superficially acquainted, no doubt to the disgust of visitors.

And visitors we had aplenty, many of them distinguished and internationally famous. During my childhood, the trip across America was still by train, and a long trip it was: a night and a day from New York to Chicago, and then two more days and nights to Spokane, at which point many people felt the urge to break the trip. The fame of the Davenport Hotel, and the spreading fame of Mother's talents as a conversationalist and cook, as well as Father's wide acquaintanceship in the world of letters, the law and state, regional and national planning, brought us a rich social life, in contrast to the bland, complacent, unintellectual, and almost wholly Republican society of Spokane.

Why, you may ask – as Mother often did – were two people of their outstanding talents supposed to be content to live in relative obscurity in this small provincial town? Father's stock answer was that most of the United States had been despoiled by willful and greedy men – damaged almost beyond repair – and that the West still had a chance to avoid the mistakes which had so damaged Europe and the rest of America. His dedication to city, county, state, and regional planning stemmed from this passionate belief. (At one time he had eleven letterheads for everything from the National Society of Planning Officials all the way down to the city planning commission; he headed all of them at one time or another, having started most of them.) His dream collapsed with the onset of World War II, when planning lost all its priorities, and the aftermath, when books such as Friedrich Hayek's *The Road to Serfdom* equated planning with socialism, which led inevitably to communism, and the death of civilization as we know it. Father never gave any indication that he realized that the West, our pristine West, was going to end up as squalid as the rest of the country. As he grew older and older, and seemed destined to live forever, I prayed that his fading sense of reality protected him from the knowledge of the worst excesses of the free-enterprise system as it tore up his beloved West.

But at any rate, his indefatigable letter writing and his passionate interest in planning and international affairs brought these streams of interesting people to our house in Browne's Addition, where they took a break before entraining for Seattle and the Pacific Coast. I will mention only a few of them, the ones who made a lasting impression on me. My husband, an architect and planner, enjoys telling people that Lewis Mumford taught me about sex. You would think that my mother the biologist might have filled me in, as she had a couple of generations of girls at Mills and San Francisco State, where she headed the departments of biology, but no. I fear that my dear mother subscribed to the fantasy that ignorance is protection. (Father coped with the whole topic in his inimitable way by pressing on me the *Collected Works* of D.H. Lawrence, which indeed I devoured, and which may have had the somewhat salutary effect of protecting me during World War II from the kinds of boys who said, "I'm shipping out tomorrow, and I may never come back." In retrospect, I wish I had honored the wholesome fears of some of them, but I was too hung up on Lawrence and what I thought of as the sanctity of sex.)

At any rate, Lewis, who had formed a fast friendship with my father through correspondence, arrived in Spokane when I was ten or so; we went out to our cabin at Hayden Lake, and in the course of taking me for a walk Lewis discovered that I knew absolutely nothing, despite Lady Chatterley (expurgated edition). He then proceeded to enlighten me – which was the last information I received until I entered college, and some kind medical students at Harvard put me to bed on their couch and dumped a comprehensive medical text on the coffee table beside me.

We had a number of Chinese visitors in those days during the Japanese invasion of Manchuria and later, the Chinese mainland; they were scouring the country's campuses to plead the Chinese cause. I remember the scholar and musicologist T. Z. Koo, a man of great beauty (and I've always been a fool for a pretty face) who wore long gowns of pale blue or grey silk, with white stockings and black cloth shoes. He usually carried a bamboo flute in his hand, and could be persuaded to perform infinitely poignant and melancholy folk airs on it. (He is also the hero of the "Likee fishee?" story which has gone round the world – and indeed his English was without flaw.) But the philosopher Dr. Hu Shih made the deepest impression on me (it's easy to tell, because I can remember speeches and conversations word for word though memory may fail me about nearly everything else).

One day we drove Dr. Hu down to Washington State College, in Pullman, a couple of hours south of Spokane. I was deeply impressed by his speech to the students and faculty because of the calm, detached tone in which he recounted the horrors of the Japanese invasion – rape, pillage, murder, destruction – and members of his own immediate family had been victims. He spoke of the necessity of stopping the Japanese, and then took a long view of how they should be treated after defeat: with the generosity of honorable men. On the way home, very emotional still, I protested, "Dr. Hu! How could you sound so calm?" "Because, my dear, it was not my own feelings I wished to arouse, but yours." I like to think that this lesson has remained with me all my life, not in my conversation – that would be too much to ask of one who inherited her mother's capacity for indignation – but in my work.

In addition to an assortment of philosophers, architects, and planners, we had a number of interesting English visitors, including Harold Laski, Vera Brittain, and Marjorie Strachey, one of Lytton's sisters. I blush to recall that when Laski inquired about the future of a politician then much in the news, I blurted out that I didn't think he could ever be successful, he was so small and he had a silly mustache, and he wore a hat that didn't fit him. As this was a dead-on description of Laski himself, I certainly didn't get any award for tact. But from what I subsequently learned of Laski, he was without tact himself, and deserved some of his own medicine. After the war, Mother and I visited Miss Brittain and her husband, George Catlin, at their home in Cheyne Walk. As shortages of almost everything were still a feature of English life in 1947, Mother had taken them a rather lavish package of tinned meat, butter, cookies, and other good things. These they refused in no uncertain terms, to my mother's deep humiliation. "As we are part of the Socialist Government which is demanding sacrifices of our people, we cannot accept gifts which would better our own lot." Speaking of tactlessness, I wondered why they hadn't just thanked Mother for her thoughtfulness and then quietly given away the food to the hungry. I think I began to believe that tactlessness was a prominent feature of British Socialism.

I remember Miss Strachey less well, perhaps because we didn't see her again after that initial visit. But I do remember that she subsequently sent me a set of the novels of Thomas Hardy. By a piece of bad luck, I began with *Jude the Obscure,* and like so many others before me, when I reached the part about the hangings in the attic, I threw the book across the room. Now if she had sent me the poetry.... But in addition to these visitors – our lifeline to the outside world – we had a guest for whom my father was responsible for a number of years. In the spring of the year after I was born, Vachel Lindsay ran an ad in a literary review inquiring, in Vachel's often inflated and dramatic style, if there was anyone out there who would care to exchange bread for poems. My father at once answered in the affirmative – and I believe his was the only response which Vachel received. Father enclosed a train ticket (coach) from Gulfport, Mississippi, to Spokane, Washington. Vachel packed up his hundreds of books, notebooks, scrapbooks, and manuscripts in Gulfport and in Springfield, Illinois, and shipped them to the Davenport Hotel. Privately, Father had made an arrangement with Louis Davenport, sole owner and proprietor, to house Vachel in a pleasant suite of rooms on the top floor, charging him the nominal sum of thirty-five dollars a month, Father to contribute the rest from his own slender pocketbook, unbeknownst to Vachel.

It is worth a moment's digression to speak of Louis Davenport, an unusual man even if this were all we knew about him. In the great Spokane fire of 1889, which virtually destroyed the city, young Louis Davenport (I believe that that was not his name then; it was something Armenian) had set up a tent and a flapjack stand on one of the ruined blocks and was doing a thriving business feeding the inhabitants, including miners, lumbermen, their families, prostitutes, and assorted scalawags. Legend has it – Mr. Davenport's legend anyhow – that a gypsy fortune-teller showed up and insisted on reading his palm. "You will be *vairy* rich and successful," she said, rolling her gypsy eyes, "if you build a hotel on this *vairy* spot, so long as your hotel is filled with singing birds, living fish, water fountains, and fresh flowers."

And so it came to pass. The Davenport was an amazing establishment for the small-town America of that day. As I was growing up, it was in its prime: Between the pillars in the lobby were hung cages of beautiful singing canaries; fires burned all day in the massive fireplaces at either end of the lobby; and in the center was a large fountain surrounded by masses of living blooms. (It is significant that the hotel prospered until Mr. Davenport died, the hotel was sold, and a series of subsequent owners eliminated the birds, the fountain, the flowers, the fish in their tanks, and the fires in the fireplaces. And the hotel, growing ever shabbier, has been in trouble ever since.)

When Vachel moved into the Davenport, all coins that passed through the hotel were washed and polished until they gleamed like new. Every incoming guest received flowers and a basket of fruit. Vachel brought with him one of his own large paintings, entitled *The Tree of Laughing Bells,* which Louis Davenport hung in a prominent place on his elegant mezzanine.

Every Sunday morning my father would walk from our house at 202 Coeur d'Alene, right at the end of Second Street, all the way down to the hotel, where he would pick up Vachel. They would walk for hours, along the banks of the Spokane River, or on the Rimrock, overlooking the valley. Vachel, an enthusiast if there ever was one, was at this time infatuated with the architect and medievalist Ralph Adams Cram, and Cram's concept of "the walled town," a utopian city whose ramparts would shut out invaders. Vachel fancied that Spokane, surrounded by rocks and scrub pine and fields, could be such a town. Vachel had had his dreams of Springfield, his hometown, but they had come to nothing. Now, perhaps, if Spokane could be made to listen to Vachel as he preached his Gospel of Beauty to men's clubs, the Elks, the Chamber of Commerce—whose program directors, always desperate for luncheon speakers, particularly those who charged no fee, were happy to invite Vachel to speak—if Spokane could be made aware of Beauty, then she might approach the ideal of Cram's and Vachel's fantasies.

When I was barely able to toddle I sometimes accompanied the two

men. There are snapshots of the three of us in the family album, Carolyn self-consciously holding up one Mary Jane-shod foot. Vachel had
told me that I had "Della Robbia toes." I had no idea what kind of toes
these were but they sounded special, so special that I thought they
might be visible through my shoes. The snapshots help to restore my
memories (though I believe that they also suppress the genuine visions
in favor of the printed ones). But I truly remember Vachel's great gusts
of laughter; it was an extraordinarily loud, braying laugh that must
have echoed for miles across the valley – and his nonstop, uninterrup-
tible discourse. What a talker the man was! I have noted with indignation that some accounts refer to Vachel as a drinker. Nothing could be
further from the truth. Like Father, he never took a drink in his life.
But unlike Ben Kizer, Vachel never outgrew his puritan origins. It's
understandable that people might think that he drank, because he became intoxicated by his own language: his voice would rise and rise
until he was shouting. I don't remember many of the words, but I will
remember the tones until death silences all.

One night Percy Grainger came to the house. He had known my father for some time, Father being chairman of the symphony board and
responsible for booking the artists who appeared with it. It was always
exciting to have Percy visit. Like Vachel, he was a highly dramatic,
even florid, personality, though far more attractive than Vachel, who
was, in truth, a plain and gawky man. Vachel believed that these qualities made him resemble his idol, Lincoln, though it is difficult for an
objective outsider to see the resemblance. Percy would appear for dinner, dazzling in white tie and tails before his concert, and would insist
on clearing off the table between courses. Percy protested his demo-
cratic spirit in all things, to the consternation of a succession of German maids who would fall back against the walls when Percy swept
into the kitchen with a pile of plates.

On this particular night, Vachel, Percy, and my parents had been to
a lecture by a young Englishman who had recently returned from Af-
rica, where he had studied tribal drumming. He came back with them
to the house, and I was permitted to come downstairs in my Doctor
Dentons because my mother believed that children should be included
in Special Occasions, which were more important in forming the infant
sensibility than Regular Hours. There was an enormous fire blazing on

the hearth, and the young Englishman was sitting crosslegged in front of it with an assortment of drums. I remember his quiet voice as he began softly, tentatively, to drum. Suddenly, Percy sprang to the piano and began to play his "Zanzibar Suite," recently composed. In a moment Vachel leapt up and began his chanting:

> Then I saw the Congo, creeping through the black,
> Cutting through the jungle with a golden track. . . .

All the lights had been turned out, and Vachel's face blazed in the firelight:

> Mumbo-Jumbo will hoo-doo you,
> Mumbo-Jumbo will hoo-doo you,
> Mumbo-Jumbo . . . will hoo . . . doo . . . you.

All my life I have lugged an old blue silk hatbox from one to another of the places I have lived. In it, along with my grandmother's, my mother's, and my own christening gown and other antique treasures, is a tiny Bible. In it, Vachel has inscribed, in his characteristic scrawl, large, round, and black, "To Carolyn, from the man who usually writes on barn doors, but can write on an angel's penny." And somewhere in every house I have owned are some framed drawings, product of Vachel's "word game." This entailed Vachel writing out the signature of the person in question, and then turning that signature into a portrait. My favorite is Elizabeth Barrett Browning, ringlets and all, a dead likeness. Vachel would have loved to have been an artist, and he kept coming back to drawing for all of his fevered life. But his gifts in this genre were limited, and most successful when linked to literature, as with the word games.

I think that people have been inclined to overestimate Vachel's influence on my becoming a poet. I think that from a very early age I sensed Vachel as a man frighteningly flawed, a man stubborn, obsessed, blind to the realities of the crass American towns where he sang his songs and preached his beliefs, whose citizens laughed at him and thought him a buffoon. And who ultimately destroyed him. No, the chief influence came from another direction. Vachel had a sister named Olive

Wakefield, a missionary in China. I remember Vachel reading her letters aloud; I remember Mother saying that Vachel wrote what was, to
her, his best poem, "The Chinese Nightingale," on our living-room
sofa. I remember Mother reading aloud to me the translations of Arthur Waley. Through Mother, and Vachel, and Mrs. Wakefield, whom
I never knew except through the excitement which her letters caused, I
acquired my unending devotion to Chinese poetry.

Of course, Vachel was a limited poet, limited in some of the ways in
which Sandburg was, and for some of the same reasons: they were
both obsessed with the idea of being American, a kind of crippling
chauvinism which blinded them to the importance of what was happening in Europe: the French symbolists, Eliot, Pound. But even with
his limitations of judgement, and I suppose ultimately, of talent, I often
wonder what Vachel's life would have been like if he had been born
forty years later. By the time he was grown, the Main Street Babbitry
of small-town America would have diminished; poets no better than he
would read poetry to jazz in San Francisco clubs to wild acclaim.

Vachel was the precursor of Dylan Thomas, to whom all poets owe
everlasting gratitude for making popular our chief source of income:
poetry readings. At his best, the companion for children, the child that
was and is me, Vachel was a magic man. My own children demanded
that I play Burl Ives singing Vachel's poems, over and over until the records were worn out: "The moon's the North Wind's cookie / he bites
it day by day . . . " Singing:

> There was a little turtle
> He lived in a box
> He swam in a puddle
> He climbed on the rocks
>
> He snapped at a mosquito
> He snapped at a flea
> He snapped at a minnow
> And he snapped at me.
>
> He caught the mosquito
> He caught the flea

He caught the minnow
But he didn't catch me.

I remember Vachel's answer to a reporter who asked him how long he
planned to stay at the Davenport. "Till the ants carry me out grain by
grain through the keyhole," he said.

And I remember standing by his knee as Vachel almost whispered
these words to me:

I heard a cricket's cymbals play,
A scarecrow lightly flapped his rags,
And a pan that hung by his shoulder rang,
Rattled and thumped in a listless way,
And now the wind in the chimney sang...

"Life is the west-going dream-storm's breath,
Life is a dream, the sigh of the skies,
The breath of the stars, that nod on their pillows
With their golden hair mussed over their eyes."
The locust played on his musical wing,
Sang to his mate of love's delight.
I heard the whippoorwill's soft fret.

I heard a cricket carolling,
I heard a cricket carolling,
I heard a cricket say: "Good-night, good-night,
Good-night, good-night...good-night."

IN AN EARLY POEM OF MINE called "By the Riverside" (the only
poem, so far as I know, that takes its epigraph from the cover of the
telephone directory: "Do not call from Memory. All numbers have
changed"), I speak of the house where I grew up, at 202 Coeur
d'Alene. For many years the house had been owned by a Dutch bank,
and passed from one bank president to the next, along with a hefty sum
for remodelling. So wings were added, rooms closed off (for example,
there was a fascinating closet five feet off the floor, about ten feet deep,
with a stained glass window at the end; Mother kept rolls of wallpaper

and carpeting in it), and windows cut through walls. Mother said that, architecturally, it was a stew. But for a child growing up, it was a dream of a house. Those mysterious corridors, that peculiar back staircase, those deep and multitudinous closets! It was always a stimulus to a burgeoning imagination, and has continued to haunt my dreams.

The Freudian belief that an old house symbolizes Mother seems just right to me (although like many another woman, I check out when it comes to Freud's theories concerning women; however, penis envy to females of my generation meant that if you had one, you too could be a Rhodes Scholar or visit Mt. Athos). Perhaps especially so in my case because my mother was old, old enough to be my grandmother: haunted, mysterious, full of hidden passages and unexpected adventures. Every Hallowe'en, from the age of five or so, I was given a party. The most wonderful feature of this event was Mother, dressed as a gypsy, telling our fortunes, and at some point leading all the little children, blindfolded, up and down and around the house. It was an extraordinary experience, being totally lost and disoriented in one's own home. I've always blessed my luck in growing up there, with her, instead of in a box-shaped tract house or an apartment.

Hallowe'en wasn't the only occasion we celebrated. Virtually every notable day on the calendar (with the exception of Mother's Day, which my mother viewed with contempt, as do I) was commemorated in some fashion, and always by handmaking something; May baskets on May Day, filled with a handful of limp flowers and weeds gathered by my grubby fingers and then hung on the doorknobs of the neighbors. Easter! My first poem written on my own, I believe, without an assist from Mother. It was sent to Bishop Cross, with whom I was in love from the age of seven or so. This early passion had something to do with the way his face reminded me of the high-laced shoes that he and my father wore, and I too at times, for weak ankles. The poem was intended as a strictly personal communication, and I was unspeakably shocked when Bishop Cross read it aloud from the pulpit on Easter Sunday. (The only line in it which had any merit at all compared the Easter lily to the angel who appeared at Christ's grave.) No one, especially the bewildered Bishop, could understand why I wasn't pleased by the publicity.

Perhaps this is the time to say a word about Religion. My father was descended from Quaker stock who became converted to Methodism late in the nineteenth century. I remember when I saw the film of Jessamyn West's *Friendly Persuasion:* there was a scene in the Quaker meetinghouse when the little children, in the dead silence of the service, heard the enthusiastic singing of the Methodists down the road, and leaned wistfully out the window. So that was how it happened! Thanks to his mother's training, my father knew the Bible backwards and forwards, and could quote Scripture verbatim. One of the delights of my childhood was listening to my father's up-to-date version of the plagues of Moses. They were deliciously funny, and I begged for them over and over again, correcting him when he altered or omitted a word until he became heartily sick of them. (Neither of my parents, skilled raconteurs, could understand why I never tired of hearing their stories.) These stories obviously influenced my artistic life: one of my early paintings is of the house where Peter's wife's mother lay sick of a fever. It shows a small contemporary cottage painted blue, with a Ford flivver parked neatly beside it.

However, by the time I came along, Father had ceased being a Methodist, or anything else, although I believe that he still believed in God, and believed in Jesus as leader, poet, and prophet. The chief remnant of his early training was song. Father had a high, thin, Methodist tenor, and when he was feeling especially pleased with life he would break into a doleful hymn tune. Mother loved to tell how, on their honeymoon, he kept singing, "How tedious and tasteless the hours / Since Jesus no longer I see, / Sweet prospects, sweet birds, and sweet flowers / Have *all* lost their sweetness for me." Mother was a nominal Episcopalian, although from time to time, feeling dissatisfied, she would try something else. I wrote about it long ago:

> For awhile my mother was a believer in Coué
> so as a child I chanted, "Every day
> in every way, I am getting better and better."

> Later in my youth
> Mother moved on to The Church of Truth

which Mrs. Weinstein led, and at her nod
we sang, "Be still and know that I am God . . . "

But both parents were deeply devoted to the Right Reverend Edward
Makin Cross, Episcopal Bishop of the enormous diocese of central and
eastern Washington, Idaho, and Montana, as I recall. He was involved
in a consuming life work: to build a Gothic cathedral designed by the
architect Harold Whitehouse on a hill in Spokane. Although I had not
been attending Sunday School, it was brought to his attention that I
was praying a good deal (a habit I have never lost), and that he was
prominently featured in those prayers. A letter from him at that time
reads in part, "Of course, we have to remember as we pray that God's
'no' is just as much an answer to prayer as is God's 'yes,' so always the
central theme of our petitions must be, 'Thy will be done.'"

It was about then that he had a serious talk with my parents, in
which he pointed out that not sending me to Sunday School was really
depriving me of choice, not giving me the freedom they intended. I
had to know what I was rejecting before I could intelligently reject it.
This argument, worthy of a Jesuit, proved compelling, and I was duly
baptized, with the Bishop and his wife as my godparents – and I've
been an Episcopalian ever since! I have two dear writer friends who go
to church along with me: George Garrett and Denise Levertov, whose
father was a converted Anglican clergyman. I don't think that the three
of us would care to be grilled on just what articles of the Nicene Creed
we accept. Let's just say that in a world of increasing chaos and violence – or perhaps one should say, "of chaos and violence that we know
about" – the stately order of the service is a solace and comfort. And,
like my dear father, I love to sing hymns! But I must say that the new
Prayer Book, which has mucked up the lovely old cadences without any
substitution of clarity, is an abomination to a faithful lover of language,
and its ubiquity has cut down on my church attendance, alas. If only
the church had listened to Wystan Hugh Auden!

Speaking of Auden, we had in common the fact that the first book
either of us was given was *Come Hither*, edited by Walter de la Mare.
My copy was presented on January 3, the day I was named. Perhaps it
was in being read to from that winsome book that I learned the name

of Thomas Love Peacock. At any rate, I fell in love with that combination of words and sounds, and used to sit on the potty shouting, "Thomas Love Peacock! Thomas Love Peacock!" a production number which I have recorded in a poem called, "What Was in a Name." But more than de la Mare's anthology I loved his "children's poems" (unaccountably omitted from his *Collected Poems*), and I still do:

> Ann, Ann!
>   Come! quick as you can!
> There's a fish that TALKS
>   In the frying pan.
> Out of the fat
>   As clear as glass
> He put up his mouth
>   And moaned 'Alas!' . . .

>   *   *   *

> Has anybody seen my Mopser? –
> A comely dog is he,
> With hair the color of Charles the Fifth
> And teeth like ships at sea;
> His tail it curls straight upwards,
> His ears stand two abreast,
> And he answers to the simple name of Mopser
> When civilly addressed.*

>   *   *   *

> 'Come!' said old Shellover.
> 'What?' says Creep.
> 'The horny old Gardener's fast asleep;
> The fat cock Thrush
> To his nest has gone,
> And the dews shine bright
> In the rising Moon;
> Old Sallie Worm from her hole doth peep;
> Come!' said old Shellover.
> 'Ay!' said Creep.

* *from* "The Bandog" by Walter de la Mare. Quoted by permission of the Literary Trustees of Walter de la Mare and the Society of Authors as their representative.

*   *   *

It's a very odd thing –
As odd as can be –
That whatever Miss T. eats
Turns into Miss T. . . .

I know a little cupboard
With a teeny tiny key,
And there's a jar of Lollypops
   For me, me, me. . . .

I have a small fat grandmama
With a very slippery knee,
And she's the Keeper of the Cupboard
With the key, key, key. . . .

*   *   *

'Grill me some bones,' said the Cobbler,
  'Some bones, my pretty Sue;
I'm tired of my lonesome with heels and soles,
Springsides and uppers too;
A mouse in the wainscot is nibbling;
A wind in the keyhole drones;
And a sheet webbed over my candle, Susie,
  Grill me some bones!'

Irresistible poems! How sad that today's children are deprived of their magic and mysteriousness. Although that most haunting of de la Mare's poems in *Peacock Pie* has come to the attention of one or two younger people. When I read Michael Ryan's poem "Gangster Dreams" not long ago, I said to him "Aha! You've imitated de la Mare's 'Song of the Mad Prince'!" and he was a little surprised that someone had spotted his homage to an obscure piece.

Mother kept a record of my reading up until the age of eight, and in addition to some of the usual children's books of that day there are many volumes of poetry and poem anthologies. But the name of Gertrude Stein does not appear there, although a poem of hers was, I believe, the first work which I had by heart – called "Grass":

Be cool inside the mule,
Be cool inside the mule,
Be cool inside, with a monkey tied,
Be cool inside the mule.

As you see, it entailed no great feats of memorization. In the meantime, Father had been reading me Kipling's stories, all of Jane Austen, and a great deal of poetry, especially his favorites, Poe and Keats. Father read aloud in a voice that throbbed with feeling. It made Mother nervous. She would jump up from her sewing at the slightest excuse, and make her escape, while Father remarked, "Mabel! Can't you sit still for a few minutes?" I've referred before to my father as "the last of the red-hot romantics." I suppose his demanding life at the office and at the bar didn't allow much scope for the deeply ardent side of his nature, that ardor which, among other things, made him always a passionately loving husband.

Even very early on I believe I preferred my mother's style. Along with Arthur Waley's translations, she read me a great deal of Robinson Jeffers (whom I think she had known slightly in her California days) and even more Whitman. My mother had the most beautiful voice, creamy, deep, and resonant; she didn't need and didn't attempt histrionics. I didn't much care for Poe, and it wasn't till later that I realized that it was his mechanical rhythms and his Gothic sentimentality that repelled me. (It was clear to me by the time I was in the eighth grade, when the teacher required everyone in the class to memorize a poem. They nearly all chose quatrains: the shortest works they could find. But a classmate, Jack, and I memorized the whole of "The Raven," which we used as an accompaniment to a soft-shoe shuffle.) Keats seemed very beautiful and very alien, and I wished that Father's reading didn't make me as uncomfortable as Mother was. Perhaps I sensed that Keats was a poet I could not emulate. Now the letters would have been a different matter, but I probably wasn't ready for them.

As a child, I suffered from severe allergies: asthma, hay fever, and eczema. Much of the time when Father read aloud, I was flaked out on the living-room sofa, trying to be as passive as possible, and concentrating on breathing. I am sure that part of Mother's and my discomfort was our sense that Father, quite unconsciously, was attempting seduction – verbal seduction to be sure – but even so, damaging I have no doubt. It must have been particularly trying for my mother, who was so extraordinarily intuitive, and a seething mass of insecurities as well. She often referred to the intellectual bond between my father and myself, as if she, poor inferior creature, were shut out. I did my best to disabuse her of this nonsense. For one thing, she was certainly our intellectual equal, surely our imaginative superior, and – far more important – my deepest bond was always with her.

Around eight I launched into serious reading. (I have a typed list, again, which my mother kept.) Mother loved to tell of finding Shaw's *Mrs. Warren's Profession* under the bathmat in the toilet, where, like many children, I had gone to find much-needed privacy. Of course she realized that I didn't have the faintest idea of the situation on which the plot turned. But at that point I was so infatuated with the way that Shaw's mind worked that I could put up with a good deal of incomprehensibility. Mother's list of my favorite plays, made when I was twelve, includes most of Shaw, seven plays of Barrie, three of Milne, and Pirandello's *The Play's the Thing*. I had been putting on plays for some time, my own, and scenes from works I admired. Mother (of course) saved the program from a production when I was eleven, which consisted of the balcony scene from *Romeo and Juliet,* a "Vaudville" (dancing dolls which I had made out of large tassels), *Portrait of a Gentleman in Slippers* (Milne), and "Walt Disney Cartoon & Poetry Reading (if we have time)."

Mother's comment at the foot of the program: "This was killing! – and extraordinary at the same time. The only audience was Ben and me and the maid whom C. insisted on coming, and rows of dolls and paper dolls. She made all the stage settings. The one for the balcony scene was lovely. Dolls took all the parts and Carolyn recited the lines behind a screen, almost all from memory."

Activities such as these prompted Mother to have a real stage built for me in the basement. She also provided a trunk full of marvelous clothes and props – including a big, blue, ostrich-plume fan which I still have: swathes of velvet and chiffon, bits of fringe, embroidery, and all sorts of exotic headgear from Mother's colorful premarital past. Of course with this kind of encouragement and equipment I was off and running. I pressed the neighborhood children into acting, ready or not, under my imperious direction.

This may be the moment to point out that, in case it has not already been made clear, my peers did not find me adorable, unlike a few adults, particularly my parents and a few selected teachers and tolerant friends of the family. The few friends I had I ruled by tyranny and bribes (Mother's cooking, Mother's parties, Mother's inventive ideas for having fun), by what I felt was the Divine Right of the spoiled only child. My only close friend in early childhood lived across the street; her name was Virginia Marshall, known as Bunny. For a number of years I bullied Bunny to my satisfaction. Her only mild revenge was in possessing a Shirley Temple doll, frills and all, which was said to resemble her, and which my mother thought tacky. (I had ethnic dolls, Indian squaws, and – to her credit – a black baby doll named Rosy Posy which Mother had to special-order from a factory.)

One night we had had an unusual snowfall, along with heavy winds, and when I woke up I found that the wind had blown a great heap of snow up against the garage. I rushed out after breakfast and began to build an igloo. When Bunny came over later in the afternoon, I had a nice passageway carved out which led to an interior space, and I had fixed the outer and inner surfaces with water, which promptly froze. I coaxed the poor child into crawling through the tunnel to the little room, which I had furnished with a toy telephone, a dish or two, and some apples. Soon after she had entered, I sealed off the entrance with more snow and left her there. So that I am not considered a total sadist or potential murderer, it really didn't occur to me that the child would be so paralyzed with fright that she wouldn't simply knock a hole in the wall and crawl out. When I sauntered back an hour or two later, I discovered her still there and let her out, puffy-faced, weeping, and freezing. Bunny never played with me again. I missed her a great deal – rather in the way that whites missed blacks when slavery was abolished – but by her own little Emancipation Proclamation she gained my permanent respect, as walking home from school I would gaze at the hedge enclosing her yard, a hedge as impenetrable as any fortress.

But there was another friend whom I managed to keep until I left Spokane, a local character called Wild Willie Wiley. One day when I was eight, Mother found me missing, and went out on the front porch, where she saw this young person with a white-blond "boyish bob" sitting on the front seat of a rattletrap open car, an Overland, next to a nearly naked man with a long bushy beard, wearing only a singlet of bobcat fur. Many a mother would have freaked out at this spectacle, and indeed Willie spent a lot of his time in jail, having been run in by parents who failed to understand the fascination that this harmless man had for children to whom he was always generous and kind. My mother was made of stronger stuff; and her intuitions told her that I had nothing to fear. Willie had been sickly in his youth, and had taken up semi-nudity as a way of building up his strength. And indeed he was solid as a rock, with a deep, leathery tan the year round. When Willie died in 1956 I am happy to say that my conservative hometown, never too kind to him while he lived, turned out for his funeral: more than three hundred people visited the funeral home, "in business suits and work clothes, in white gloves, pigtails, and bobbysox," according to a local columnist. And there is a memorial stone to Willie in a Spokane cemetery.

It didn't occur to me until just now that Willie and Vachel were soul brothers; with some similarities to my father as well, with his regimen of daily morning exercises, his nearly vegetarian diet, and his emphasis on a healthy body. And I wonder if Willie wasn't responsible in part for my continuing attraction to oddballs, free spirits, and eccentrics. In this respect, too, I was my mother's child; my father didn't really notice whether people were eccentric or not!

MOTHER MANAGED TO SNEAK ME into public school while I was still five, knowing that, with my December birthday, I would be held back a year if she waited until I was six. I attended the Washington School, a gloomy old pile so prisonlike in appearance that it haunted my dreams for years. I remember the sense of relief I felt when I awoke and realized that I was grown up! It was about fifteen long blocks from our house, and like most children I took my lunch. However, my lunches bore little resemblance to those of the other children. Describing them to friends later on, I exaggerated only marginally when I said they could consist of Breast of Chicken under Glass. Take it from me, they were gourmet all the way. Naturally, this set me apart, as did my hand-knits, my old-fashioned hair styles, and my voracious appetite for reading. Nothing could be done about the latter, but occasionally I was able to swap my exquisite and nutritionally balanced lunch for the ambrosial contents of Joey Lindsley's brown bag: a peanut-butter and jelly sandwich on Wonderbread (forbidden to our house; every Sunday we crossed the river to the aromatic bakery of the Seventh Day Adventists, to purchase our homemade bread for the week), cherry jello with bits of canned fruit and tiny marshmallows embedded in it, and a big hunk of Mrs. Lindsley's featherweight chocolate layer cake, whose memory makes me salivate right now.

Because of Mother's dread of tuberculosis, which had caused both of her parents to migrate from the South to Colorado soon after they were wed, and which had run riot through Mother's own generation, I had been scientifically over-vitaminized since birth. Daddy was just past six feet tall, and Mother five eight, very tall for her generation. So the combination of genes and systematic feeding made me always at least a head taller than my peers. I'm not hard to spot in class pictures, with my hair like a blown dandelion, in the back row, overtopping the others.

In those antediluvian days, women teachers in my State – and they were always women – lost their jobs if they married. And we were, of course, deep in the Depression. So for teachers we had a series of "old maids," none of them younger than forty, and a number of them, it was said, over seventy and dying their hair. It is remarkable how many of these women, lonely, tired and overworked – usually with an invalid mother or a feckless sibling or two to support – managed to be habitually kind, interesting, and dedicated. We had one psychopath in seventh grade, Miss Mead, who warped several generations of children before being committed to the madhouse, but the rest were, by and large, angels. Miss Odell, my first-grade teacher, had taught the mothers and grandmothers of many of my classmates, and ended up being adored by five generations.

And Miss Odell, like most of my teachers then and later, loved me back. I was reading fluently when I entered school, and I had been trained to read aloud as well. My classmates divided roughly into thirds: one-third middle-class children like me from Browne's Addition, one third from Fort Wright, the army post, and one third from Peaceful Valley, which was what passed for a slum in Spokane: a poor but pastoral enclave under the hill along the banks of the Spokane River. The army brats did fairly well in school but they took no interest in mental exercise. The poor kids, often hungry and wretchedly clothed, particularly miserable in our bitter winters, frequently had all they could do to concentrate on their lessons. Of course my teachers loved me, and like my parents, spoiled me. As far as I can recollect, I never did homework. I got up my lessons in study period, or faked my way through question periods, while beamed upon and held up as an example. Only Miss Griffith, my sixth-grade teacher, made any attempt to discipline me. I think she felt that somebody better try. And she sharply cross-questioned me at every turn, exposed me when I was bluffing, and constantly challenged me to do better work commensurate with the extraordinary advantages of my upbringing. Single-handedly she could hardly hope to reform me, but it is significant that whenever I returned to Spokane after I left for college I never failed to visit her.

Perhaps my most vivid memory of grade school is of Miss Mead. She was habitually scornful of the poor children from the Valley, although deferential to me and to Joe Lindsley, whose father was a Superior Court Judge, and to the army kids whose fathers were officers. One day she flew totally off the handle and began to berate the Valley children:

"Do you know that you're nothing but trash, the worst of trash?" she hissed, and began flailing at them with her ruler and screaming, "Trash!" over and over again. Joe Lindsley and I rose as one from our seats and told her to stop it. Then we marched into the principal's office, where she soon came panting after us. I no longer remember how the matter was settled although both Joe's and my mother became involved. There was some kind of a truce, and Joe and I were unpunished. She managed to control herself then, but I know that she went on abusing children long after Joe and I had graduated from all our schools. I still see the foam on her lips and the rictus of her terrible smile, and wonder how many lives she damaged.

The summer of 1936 was an important one for me in several ways. We attended a conference of the Institute of Pacific Relations in Yosemite, saw old friends like Dr. Hu Shih, and made new ones, particularly among the other Chinese delegates, the Russians, and the Japanese. The wife of a Chinese delegate, Mrs. Sze, gave me a ring cut from a single piece of Imperial jade which I treasured until it was stolen thirty years later. I have a snapshot of myself dressed by Mrs. Takianagi in her purple kimono. But by all means the most significant encounter was with the family of the Russian journalist Vladimir Romm, the Washington correspondent for *Isvestia*. The Romms had a little son, George, a couple of years younger than I, and the Romms and the Kizers tramped in the Yosemite woods together, fed squirrels, admired giant redwoods, and picnicked from boxes prepared by the staff of the Awahnee Hotel where we were luxuriously housed. My mother noticed and remarked on the deep and passionate bond between the senior Romms; further, she commented on Mrs. Romm's seeming anxiety about her husband. "When he goes away for an hour or two, they embrace as if they would never see each other again," Mother remarked, prophetically. Before the conference was over Romm was suddenly called back to Moscow. There ensued many tears and much frenzied packing, and the Romms departed in haste and obvious perturbation.

The following January we were horrified to learn that Vladimir Romm had been arrested, tried, and convicted in the infamous Moscow conspiracy trials. Romm had "confessed" to having been the contact man between Trotskyite conspirators in Russian and Trotsky himself. The editor of the *San Francisco Chronicle*, who had also been a delegate to the Yosemite conference, said that Mr. Romm had confessed to personal participation "in something which never happened and in which it would have been physically impossible for him to have played the part to which he has 'confessed'" [sic]. We never heard what became of him; presumably he was killed. And I never knew what became of my friend George, though I have asked many people many times over the years.

My family discussed this over and over again. Why had Romm gone back when it was obvious, in retrospect, that he was in deep trouble? Perhaps it was his clear conscience, his misplaced belief that some measure of honor and decency still pervaded the system of which he was a part. And what a price he paid for this naiveté! Interestingly enough, Vladimir Romm's naiveté served to protect my own, just a few years later, when I attended a college where a number of my teachers were Marxists and a few were communists. And some of my fellow students called themselves communists. At that time in our history you couldn't be an American Communist without sedulously following the twists and turns of Soviet policy. Stalin owned and operated American Communism, whether all members of the Party admitted it to themselves or not.

But, idealist that I was, and having vivid memories of the Depression when I was a child – apples sold on street corners, milk running in the gutters, a procession of the poor begging at our door (the screen door of our kitchen had a mysterious mark on it which we learned indicated that the lady of the house was always good for a free meal; indeed Mother kept a great big stock pot simmering on the back of the stove, to which she added meat and nourishing vegetables to fill up empty stomachs) – it would not have been unusual for me to have been tempted by communism, and its avowed mission to help the wretched of the earth. From this Romm saved me. And "socialist realism" in the arts played a part as well. When schoolmates lent me copies of the *Masses* or the *Daily Worker,* I have to confess that I found the literary and art criticism hilarious; if they were serious I was certainly not. I confess that aesthetics had played as important a part in my politics as in my religion.

Later in 1937 I received letters from China from Mr. Fred Sze and his wife, in belated answer to my own. His of September 28 tells me that Mrs. Sze and the children had left for the country just days before the Japanese attack on Shanghai, "so they have been spared the horror of a devastating war which I have been witnessing daily for the past month and a half. . . ." But the letter of this wealthy, delicate, and sheltered woman, written just before Christmas, tells of a perilous trip of three days and nights, when the Japanese bombed their train; she and the children hid under the walled gate of a city while a bomb was dropped about thirty yards away. "The detonation was truly frightful. Thank God we got thru safely!" My peaceful Spokane had been invaded by the terrors of the big world. I remember walking home from school up Second Street, with its large houses and wide green lawns, the spidery sprinklers turning lazily in the sunlight, hearing the voice of Hitler from the open windows: that harsh, hypnotic, terrifying voice pouring from each radio, so that someone who knew German would not have missed a word. And the even more terrifying, mechanical, ritual response from a hundred thousand throats: *"Sieg Heil! Sieg Heil! Sieg Heil!"*

Recently I wrote a poem in which I mentioned a "recurring nightmare" of that period which went on for some years:

> Jackboots on the stairs, the splintered door just before dawn,
> And the fascists dragging Daddy out of bed,
> Dragging him down the steps by his wonderful hair;
> The screams as his spine cracks when he hits cement.
> Then they make him brush his teeth with his own shit.
> Though I know this is the price of bravery,
> Of believing in justice and never telling lies,
> And of being Benjamin, the best beloved....

I believe that part of this dream (O, be quiet, Freudians!) had to do with my sense that my father, although possessed of great moral courage (among other acts, he had defended Americans of German ancestry who were persecuted during World War I — and remember, the villain of that war was another Kaiser), was not physically courageous — and neither am I. (So the dream would seem to be a rare example of my identification with my father.) I remember my mother's and my silent suffering at the dinner table when Father regaled us with a blow-by-blow account of his latest visit to the dentist. And the slightest scratch or wound led him to carry on as if he'd had an amputation without anaesthetic. This was in contrast to my mother's stoicism in regard to her painful ailments, both real and psychosomatic. She postponed having her gallbladder removed for a couple of years, until I was eight, believing that she might not survive the operation and anxious that I not become an orphan until I was older. She suffered excruciatingly from colitis for the rest of her life, and I don't believe that she ever slept through the night. On the occasions when I arose in the dark hours, I was often aware of her endless, lonely pacing.

Related to the postponement of her visit to the Mayo Clinic was the conflagration in the driveway in our backyard, when my mother burned every scrap of her correspondence, her journals and notebooks as well. Why? Mother had had a "past." Father had been a virgin when he married the first time, at thirty-six, and had had no other loves beside his first wife and my mother. Mother, on the other hand, had many amorous adventures, including the most serious affair of her life, in her forties before she met my father. (She used to warn me about that when I was still a child: "Watch our for your forties! If you fall in love then it can nearly kill you." Of course she was right – but who heeds such warnings? And it nearly killed me.) She was afraid that if she died, Father would go through her papers – and perhaps at a later time I would as well. I don't believe my father, the least jealous of men, would have been upset, and I know I wouldn't have been. I have never ceased to regret this erasure of her past, particularly those years of which she never spoke.

When I entered the eighth grade of the Washington School, my teacher was a spiritual and emaciated spinster (though the word is now out of fashion, it was absolutely appropriate then) named Miss Whittaker. Even the crudest children adored her; having survived Miss Mead, we were somewhat stunned by the rule of love. She wore the same dress day after day, month after month, its detachable collar and cuffs always fresh and neatly pressed. One morning she appeared in a new dress: light blue with white dots. And as one we stood up and cheered. I have not forgotten the way she blushed with pain. How terribly poor she must have been, that gallant woman.

I also remember the music period, when we listened to ancient records on a temperamental windup Victrola which tended to run down before the end of the record and howl dolefully like a wounded beagle. And we sang as well. Our repertoire consisted, in the main, of Negro Spirituals. Here we were, as far from the Old South as we could get, geographically, singing,

"All the darkies am a weepin' / Massa's in the cole, cole groun'," singing of the days when our black hearts were young and gay as we hoed that corn and cotton, of how we longed to be carried back to Ole Virginny, "where this old darkie's heart am long to go." Dear suffering Jesus! Perhaps if a single black child had attended school with us, these words might have ceased to be abstractions, and Joe and I might have led another rebellion.

Halfway through that year, my parents transferred me to Havermale Junior High School, across the river, chiefly because of the reputation of the principal, a progressive teacher receiving a great deal of attention because he had instituted what he called a "free day": Every Friday we could choose which classroom we wanted to spend time in. It worked remarkably well as I recall, at least so far as I was concerned: Being a longtime victim of "Math anxiety," and having been given the only grade lower than an A in my life in Algebra, I would work out in the mornings with my math teacher, Noble F. Leach. Until he entered my life I had equated the study of Math with a visit to the dentist. After he explained things and straightened me out, I would dash for the Art room and spend the rest of the day happily drawing and painting. My favorite, though, was Arthur Biggs, a distant relative of the late organist, for whom we sang in the chorus and in operettas. I had tiny solo parts, and I like to think that I might have had bigger starring roles had it not been for the presence of a pretty girl named Patrice Munsil who walked off with all the leads.

Most of the children at Havermale were not well-off, and I was deeply embarrassed at being driven to school in our Buick, so I made a deal with Mr. Priebe, our splendid German gardener, to take me to school in his rattletrap Model-A. I don't know that this deceived anybody, but it made me feel better. After Havermale, Patrice and I both transferred to Lewis and Clark High school, back on the right side of the river – the very same school from which my father had had to drop out as a lad. It was a huge establishment whose principal feature was the Thursday morning pep rally at which we sang fight songs and cheered on the football or basketball team, depending on the season. Occasionally these sessions featured Patrice's singing "The Bell Song," from *Lakme,* or other ambitious arias which her ambitious mother had prompted her to learn, as vital to a precocious career which began with lessons in artistic whistling.

But that summer before moving over to high school, Patrice and another, older girl named Josephine Rangan and I responded to a newspaper ad calling for chorus members for the touring San Carlo opera company which was about to perform in Spokane. Soon we were being interviewed by Maestro Colantoni, a minute Italian who seemed to be part genius-entrepreneur, part charlatan, and part the unlucky victim of circumstance. I vividly recall his account of an outdoor performance of *Aida* which perhaps terminated his career in the land of his birth. He made use of animals including elephants, and his description of the great heaps of dung which they produced, followed almost immediately by the corps de ballet, who slipped in shit, fell down, collapsed, and caused the curtain to be rung down apace was a mixture of high comedy and bitter grief. The current enterprise seemed to be put together with adhesive tape, spit, and a prayer.

But it was a glorious opportunity for us! Patrice and Josephine were cast in small roles; I lied about my age (and Patrice must have done so too) and became a member of the chorus. In *Cavelleria* I actually had two lines of my own to sing. But that was of minor importance. The great thing was learning the operas: *Carmen, Cav* and *Pag, Traviata, Trovatore.* Fifty years later, I can still sing along with *Cav* and *Pag,* and bits of *Trovatore* stick with me – but glorious *Carmen!* I can sing the whole thing, including the overture! Most of the stars of the company were, to put it bluntly, over the hill, with the possible exception of the tenor, whose handicap was that he was nearly a midget, despite his four-inch built-up heels. The baritone, however, was a figure to whom I attached my nebulous adolescent feelings. My mother found this hilarious, which wounded me deeply, as I had been wounded not long before when she laughed at my vows to remain unmarried forever. Sandro Giglio couldn't have been younger than fifty; later when I saw French films starring Jean Gabin, I recognized the type. He had the remnants of a fine voice, and he could act. All in all, it was a romantic summer, for which I bless the memory of Maestro Colantoni.

One benefit for me was to be taken into the bosom of Josephine's large Italian family, with whom I spent many happy evenings around the old upright piano, singing operas straight through, every member of her family taking part. I'm afraid I drank some homemade chianti, having helped tread the grapes for it in my bare feet. (I don't remember Mother making any comments about purple ankles. She was good about things like that.) So I had a glimpse of a very different life-style, materially poorer than our own, but full of laughter, joy, and song. Not much later, Josephine went on to the San Francisco Opera, and Patrice, at eighteen, had the spelling of her last name changed, won the Metropolitan auditions and joined the Metropolitan Opera Company.

My immediate future was far less glamorous. I've said, more or less in jest, that all I learned in high school was how to type, and that is virtually true. No science, no math, and no foreign languages. It is not surprising that I applied to Sarah Lawrence College, probably the only institution unconventional enough to accept me. My high-school graduation exercises may have had something to do with this happy outcome: As usual, I had woefully neglected my history homework, and feared that I might flunk history and fail to graduate. So for ancient Mr. Teakle, my teacher, I stayed up most of one night and wrote a poem about the necessity of American intervention in World War II. (The previous spring I had won a medal from the Veterans of Foreign Wars for an essay on "Permanent Peace for America." Prophetic I was not.) All during my school years I was surrounded by conservative children and teachers. I battled Mr. Teakle and indeed the entire class on everything to do with economics and politics. To calm the waters, our jest was that the only thing we agreed on was that Spokane needed a sewage disposal system. Now the poem, called "Stars through the Perilous Night," impressed Mr. Teakle enough to pass me, and impressed the principal sufficiently that the poem ended up being chanted by my entire graduating class during commencement. And, for an hour, I felt that I was one of them.

Someone sent the poem to the then popular journalist Dorothy Thompson, who ran part of it in her daily column. This attracted the attention of the editors of the *Ladies' Home Journal*, who ran the entire poem in the magazine, along with a picture and a brief biography of me. From this I received more than five hundred letters. (This must have totally overwhelmed my mother's curatorial impulses, for they have all disappeared.) Later, after I had been admitted to college, the poem was set to music and performed on "The Prudential Family Hour," a popular radio program, and sung by a cast of hundreds. I remember very little about this entire experience, except that it frightened me severely, as I knew I wasn't ready for all this attention. I was at least bright enough to know that as far as my writing was concerned, I didn't know what I was doing. And it wasn't for another thirteen years, until I studied with Theodore Roethke, that I found out. My writing teacher at college was Genevive Taggard, who either threw my poems in the wastebasket or suggested that I send them to a magazine. Explaining how to make a good poem out of a bad poem was quite beyond her powers. So for the next few years I had to rely on lucky accidents rather than learned skills.

In my sophomore year, however, I wrote a poem which I thought good enough to submit to the college literary magazine. Miss Liddell, the adviser, an elderly blonde with Shirley Temple ringlets, promptly rejected it. "Send it to the *New Yorker* dear," Genevive said, in her languid way; I did, and they took it. So I felt justified in going back to Miss Liddell and announcing the acceptance. "Well, we have very high standards, dear," she replied. The poem was published, and then reprinted in the overseas edition of the magazine which was sent to the armed services abroad, as we were now at war. And eventually I received another five hundred letters or so, from servicemen. (Many years later, I mentioned to the poet Ruthven Todd that I had had a poem in the *New Yorker* at age seventeen. "It wasn't very good," I said, hoping he wouldn't look it up. But he did, and announced, "You were right. It wasn't very good." So perhaps Miss Liddell was vindicated.)

I think the importance of all this was that I began, very tentatively and shyly, to think of myself as someone who might become a poet. The materials were all in place: my family, my imagination, my reading. Now all I needed was to learn how to do it. But something else of importance occurred to me when I was eighteen. It seems to confirm Erik Erikson's theory about a pivotal experience or decision which alters the course of a life. I have no idea what event or series of events, internal or external, brought this on. I only know that at this point I decided that I didn't like myself very much: I was narcissistic, selfish, and self-absorbed. Other people, their pains, delights, and problems impinged on my consciousness only peripherally. "Well, you're just going to start behaving like a nice, decent, generous human being, and if you keep it up long enough and hard enough, it will become internalized, and you will really be that person without play-acting or hypocrisy."

The interesting part about this decision was that I fully believed that major artists were, by and large, not very nice people, and that if I continued as I was, my chances of becoming a real poet were probably much better than if I embarked on this conscious campaign of self-improvement. Nevertheless, I stuck to it. Of course psychologists will say that I had deep inner doubts of my own talent; feminists will say that this was a way of avoiding competition in the ruthless world of men. My own tentative psychological interpretation is that, once again, I chose sides and once again I chose Mother rather than Father.

At my rate, riddled with self-doubt as I was, utterly bewildered about my identity (so much so that I used to joke that I was afraid to look in the mirror for fear that nobody would look back), ignorant of life and unskilled in my craft, still I was ready to fare forth. Product of my parents, and what they had told me of their parents and their beginnings, influenced by their stories, beguiled by their voices, taking my place at the end of their family myths, I was the child of their childhood as well as my own.

Everything that was to come – war, love, marriage, separation, loneliness, children, the death of those I loved – was simply going to be added on to the person I was already. Oh, eventually I would figure myself out, more or less. And in about twenty-five years I would be able to say with Chaucer's Criseyde, "I am my owne woman, wel at ese." But by then, at eighteen, the material from which I would make my poems was in my head and in my hands. The rest is encounters, episodes, and events. They can wait. . . .

The Poet as Poem:
Emily Dickinson

"WHAT HAS SHE DONE to our Emily?" I repeated to myself, in the course of reading Cynthia Griffin Wolff's critical biography of the great Dickinson (*Emily Dickinson,* Knopf, 1986). The "our" in that sentence is significant. Even those who faintly know and little understand the Amherst poet feel a curious possessiveness about her that I don't believe we entertain about any other American writer. Sentimentalists attribute this to what we have been told of her increasingly reclusive spinsterhood in the midst of a bunch of quarreling relatives in the snug and smug little town where she lived her life, the charming, intimate touching letters she wrote, and what I can only call her girlishness, untouched by age or time. But in truth it is the poems themselves that reach out to us so confidingly, the language so pure, the meaning so evanescent. All good poets give credence to our own personal interpretations of life, and Emily, more than most, can reveal our own truths to us, and then gleefully snatch them away! Take that perhaps most famous poem of Dickinson's which begins,

> The soul selects her own Society—
> Then—shuts the Door...

Now that's perfectly clear, isn't it? Isn't it?

On the cover of Dr. Wolff's book is a reproduction of the only known portrait of Emily Dickinson, the familiar, faded brown daguerreotype taken when she was seventeen or eighteen years old. But on this book jacket the portrait has been touched up—painted, in fact. Our

Emily is wearing rouge and lipstick! Now it's quite unfair to attribute to the author the faults of the book designer, as authors rarely have control over matters which publishers jealously arrogate to themselves. But here it does seem an apt metaphor for the face which Dr. Wolff has imposed on Miss Dickinson. Here is Emily according to Freud, an Emily who bristles with phallic armament, mud-wrestling with God.

A sample: In discussing poem #505, which begins, "I would not paint – a picture . . . ", and ends with the well-known lines, "Had I the art to stun myself / With Bolts of Melody," Dr. Wolff comments as follows: " . . . the climax of the poem (which is a sexual climax as well as an artistic one) can be seen as pointedly and comically paradoxical: to 'stun' oneself 'With Bolts of Melody!' is, given the highly charged sexual context, either to be masturbating or to be coupling with oneself (as hermaphrodite?)." I'm going to return to this particular poem in a moment, both to illustrate Dickinson's teasing genius which encourages a variety of interpretations – with the exception of Dr. Wolff's interpretation, the kind of coarse, reductive nonsense which one thought had gone out of style two generations ago.

But for a moment let us pause and consider the reception which Dr. Wolff's book has had: "Three printings and a burst of praise" trumpets her publisher's ad in *The New York Review of Books*. True, the critics are bursting with praise, but when you examine these carefully chosen quotes, the praise is centered on Wolff's analysis of Dickinson's historic milieu, the background – social and religious – of her parents and grandparents, her solid grounding in scripture, and the really excellent education she received, no doubt the equivalent of a Ph.D. today, at the Amherst Academy. (This last analysis is particularly important, as many critics have scanted on Emily's solid intellectual attainments and have placed her firmly in the "warbling wood-notes wild" school of poets.) All well and good, and if Dr. Wolff had been content with that, we would all be in her debt. I can conclude two things about the comments of the critics: first, that they never delved deeply into this book of formidable length, and only absorbed the first few chapters (a habit not uncommon among harried book-reviewers working against a deadline); and second, none of the reviewers cited is a poet or has any particular background in poetry as a critic or teacher. The danger is, of course, that naive students (is there any other kind these days?) and adult readers trying to acquire a little more aid in interpreting this wonderfully difficult work will swallow Dr. Wolff's Emily, and, if not repelled by Emily as she is painted, will embrace a far less complex and mesmerizing genius.

Now let us consider the full text of poem #505:

> I would not paint – a picture –
> I'd rather be the One
> It's bright impossibility
> To dwell – delicious – on –
> And wonder how the fingers feel
> Whose rare – celestial – stir –
> Evokes so sweet a Torment –
> Such sumptuous – Despair –
>
> I would not talk, like Cornets –
> I'd rather be the One
> Raised softly to the Ceilings –
> And out, and easy on –
> Through Villages of Ether –
> Myself endued Balloon
> By but a lip of Metal –
> The pier to my Pontoon –
>
> Nor would I be a Poet –
> It's finer – own the Ear –
> Enamored – impotent – content –
> The License to revere,
> A privilege so awful
> What would the Dower be,
> Had I the Art to stun myself
> With Bolts of Melody!

In her long analysis of this poem (more than five pages) Dr. Wolff makes one of her good intuitive remarks when she says that Dickinson's family were unable to comprehend "that her art originated in a metaphysical imperative – not in mere lachrymose sensibility." If Dr. Wolff had kept that metaphysical imperative more firmly in mind, she would have saved us all a great deal of grief (and hilarity, I must confess). But most of the time she doesn't make the distinction between Religion, Metaphysics and Mysticism (to adopt Emily's system of capitalization for a moment). As Louise Bogan has so wisely emphasized, Emily Dickinson was a mystical poet – although I prefer to think of her as a metaphysical poet in the great tradition of the Psalmists, the authors of the King James Bible, George Herbert and John Donne, through William Blake, whose deceptively simple prosody, especially in "Songs of Innocence and Experience," seems a precursor of Emily's own. And she is firmly in the tradition of George Herbert in her "adaptation of a complex scheme of ancient emblems that can still speak poignantly . . . " (That quote is Dr. Wolff's – another signpost down a road she has not taken . . .)

Christian emblems – symbols and pictures so familiar to assiduous Bible-readers, as Amherst inhabitants were – were frowned upon by the Congregational church which the Dickinsons attended. But we know that Emily – deprived of the parables in stained glass that inspired George Herbert – found emblems, even as a child, in copies of Quarles's *Emblems, Divine and Moral* with "elegant plates," and books such as *Religious Emblems* and *Religious Allegories* (this information thanks to Dr. Wolff). As Wolff remarks in a note, Dickinson's appropriation of religious conventions is very like Donne's. The comparison of a Biblical type to a contemporary Christian was a commonplace in Dickinson's time:

"A type is some outward or sensible thing ordained of God under the Old Testament, to represent and hold forth something of Christ in the New" – Increase Mather's "The Figures and Types of the Old Testament." In another note, Wolff quotes Barbara Lewalski: "In the private sphere the same two formulas were available for relating the contemporary Christian to the Biblical type." From there it is a small step to relate the Biblical type to the contemporary poet, for a literary genius like Dickinson. It is this step which, over and over again, Wolff fails to make. She seems unable to get it through her head that the traditional emblems and types which Dickinson manipulates are *metaphors* of what is already symbolic. Thus, in our cited poem, Wolff says that the "odd assortment of body parts" (fingers, lip, ear) "recalls God's assault upon the coherent 'I' that begins with a demand for faith and submission to conversion, and that culminates in an extinction of self which is death...." Does this seem to have any relevance to the poem under consideration?

Maybe the good part of an interpretation like this is that it gives, unwittingly, the intelligent reader permission to make her or his own interpretation of the poem no matter how far-out or subjective it may be. After all, among its other functions, poetry is supposed to be *fun* – for reader as well as writer.

To encourage even more freedom in making your own meaning, let's look at what Adrienne Rich says about #505 (as quoted by Dr. Wolff): "This poem is about choosing an orthodox 'feminine role'.... The receptive rather than the creative; viewer rather than painter, listener rather than musician; acted-upon rather than active.... The strange paradox of this poem – its exquisite irony – is that it is about choosing not to be a poet...." Dr. Wolff more or less agrees with this view of the poem, although she insists on its "high comedic tone." Now, eager as I am to find the fun in poetry, I think this is a passionately serious poem. And, contrary to my esteemed friend, Ms. Rich, I believe that this poem says, "I don't want to paint a picture; I want to be a *painting*. I don't was to be a musical instrument; I want to be the *song*. I don't want to be a poet; I want to be the POEM!" And this poem ends with such a terrific poem that it knocks itself out.

Meanwhile, Dr. Wolff is preoccupied with more Freud-babble: "Cornets is... an instrument of music, a horn; it is also 'an officer of cavalry' – thus are song and warfare concisely combined. Moreover, while 'horn' recalls the male sexual organ, to one who speaks 'New Englandly' the cornet is also that horn of plenty, the cornucopia of the Thanksgiving feast – fruit-filled harvest pouring from a container fashioned in a patently sexual configuration, the female organs in the process of birthing." Later on, Wolff comments: "Dickinson affirms the *physical* differences between the sexes. [Huh?] 'To 'wonder how the fingers feel / Whose rare – celestial – stir – / Evokes so sweet a Torment – ' is perhaps, to be a woman aroused, pleased with erotic stimulation and simultaneously curious about the feelings of her partner...." [Uh-huh.]

Now let me just posit that the fingers are the fingers of the Muse-poet; Emily Dickinson *is* the poem on the page who is being fingered, like someone picking out a tune (on a cornet, if you will); like someone revising her, the poem; like a Galatea who is simultaneously her own Pygmalion, her own creation-creator. Like, in fact, our own elusive complicated Emily who, like all of our great loves, forever tantalizes, and forever escapes us. Just read the poems. Your guesses are as good as mine. We are all of us right and all of us mistaken – and somewhere Emily Dickinson is secretly smiling.

The Muse that Flew Away:
Louise Bogan

No ONE IN THIS CENTURY—perhaps no one since the seventeenth century—has written the pure lyric with more skill, grace and brilliance than Louise Bogan. That her output was relatively slight should not affect our judgment. We acknowledge the genius of Sappho, although we possess only fragments of her poetry. When, not so long ago, we had only a handful of Emily Dickinson's poems – and these whimsically and clumsily altered by her successive heirs and editors—we were assured of her genius as, by her own test: The hair rose on the napes of our necks. After hundreds of readings – for I have taught Bogan for fifteen years, used her, that is, to teach people how to write – I read again lines such as:

> Come, break with time,
> You who were lorded
> By a clock's chime . . .

My body as well as my brain knows that I am in the presence of the real, true thing. But, like caviar or truffles, Bogan should be savored in small portions. To read all of Bogan at a sitting induces Weltschmerz and melancholy. And the poems that breathe world-weariness, and ache with renunciation and the onset of age are the work of a young woman. In the last thirty years of her life, her output dwindled down to a handful of poems, and then she fell silent.

In her foreword to *Louise Bogan: A Portrait* (Knopf, 1985), Elizabeth Frank says, "Something stopped Louise Bogan dead in her tracks, not once, but many times." It is the aim of this fine and sensitive biography to discover why.

When I met Louise, I was a young woman and she was in her midfifties, still handsome, still, insofar as another woman can know, sexually attractive. Although her hair was dark, she gave the impression of fairness, with her creamy Irish skin, accented by the black velvet band she habitually wore around her hair. She was large, commanding, utterly poised, able to imbibe vast quantities of drink without showing a thing. If ever a woman seemed in full possession of herself, it was Louise.

When she read her work aloud, she pronounced each syllable with deliberation, and with what used to be called "pear-shaped tones." Clearly she knew the weight and value of every word: "It is a hollow garden, under the cloud; / Beneath the heel a hollow earth is turned . . ." I can hear her now, pearls dropping from her lips, as the old fairy tales would have it.

One evening, Louise and Stanley Kunitz were sitting by the fire in my study in Seattle, drinks in hand, when Louise sighed deeply and said she wished she knew a woman to go to Europe with her. "Hell, Louise," Stanley said, "why don't you go with a man?" Flattered but reproachful, she said that was all long behind her. Sex, and all that. Even to someone like myself, younger than her daughter, this seemed vaguely preposterous, as it did to Kunitz. But in this attitude she was quite consistent with her poetry, even that of twenty years before.

Little did I suspect, then, the passion that had animated that woman's breast! Oh, I had heard malicious rumors of an affair with a "fur thief" many, many years earlier; and I knew that she was still listed in the New York telephone directory as "Mrs. Raymond Holden," although she and Holden had been divorced for over twenty years — which seemed to indicate a lingering attachment to him.

Now Frank makes clear it was that passionate nature that nearly destroyed her, and her repeated attempts to kill her own deep feelings seem to have killed the poems that lay within her.

In her childhood, Louise was shunted from a series of hotel rooms and boardinghouses to homes briefly occupied, loud with quarrels and rancor. Her father seems to have been something of a cipher. We get no clear picture of him, but that's not Frank's fault. One wonders if Louise really knew him or really cared about him. The engagement, the passion, the pain all center in her relations with her mother. Her earliest memories involve scenes of violence:

"Lamplight, an open trunk, its curved lid thrown back, in the middle of the room. Her mother bends over the trunk, folding things, crying and screaming. Her father is somewhere in the shadows, and he groans as if he had been hurt. The terrified child, swept into her mother's arms and carried out of the room, knows that her mother is running away . . ."

"May Bogan had lovers – men she called 'admirers' – and assignations with them for which she spent hours bathing and dressing and putting on rice powder and fresh underclothes and earrings. In the journals, Louise remembers: 'The door is open, and I see a ringed hand on the pillow; I weep by the hotel window as she goes down the street, with another . . .'"

"Why did May Bogan take her child along to her trysts? Was it folly, or 'pure' Victorian ignorance which allowed her to think that whatever sexual goings-on Louise might chance to see or hear would pass over her head or be easily explained away?"

No wonder, then, that Louise at nineteen, offered a scholarship at Radcliffe, dropped out to marry an army captain, from whom she was separated little more than a year later, though she had his child by then. A year after that, the captain conveniently died, thus saving Louise the trouble of divorcing him, and making her eligible for a widow's pension. By then Louise was, "in her own fastidious way a Greenwich Village Bohemian," as Frank remarks. Her daughter was parked with her parents, and Louise was rapidly becoming the darling of an interesting literary set.

Her first book of poems, *Body of This Death,* was published in 1923, and she met Raymond Holden, an attractive, amiable minor poet and future novelist of sorts, who was to be the passion of her life. Even before they were free to marry, Louise's long torture of herself, and him, began. Somehow, her memories of her mother's infidelities aroused in her a pathological sexual jealousy. The storms, the scenes, the irrational accusations continued for years, before and after their marriage.

I feel more sympathy for poor Holden than does author Frank. The man put up with behavior that would have led most men to slam the door after about two weeks. Like most people who are hysterically accused of repeated infidelities without a scrap of proof, Holden eventually justified her terrors.

After great agony of mind, Louise divorced him in 1934, whereupon Raymond promptly married the lady into whose arms he had been driven and lived, so far as we know, happily ever after.

Louise wrote, "It is yourself whom you love—and it is a love given where it should be given, after years of choosing the wrong object... As for wanting someone—no. There can be no new love at thirty-seven, in a woman. So let there be no pretense of there being any." So began her long and often losing struggle to subdue her passionate nature and control her pain.

Frank quotes her marvelous, numb and dirge-like lyric, "Simple Autumnal," which bears "the burden of unreleased, shored-up emotion..."

> The measured blood beats out the year's delay.
> The tearless eyes and heart, forbidden grief,
> Watch the burned, restless, but abiding leaf,
> The brighter branches arming the bright day...

Frank goes on to say that, "this stupor that arrests life appears as the refusal to mourn, a perverse defiance of that process Freud called 'grief-work,' whereby painful memories must be reexperienced, and relinquished."

Louise spent the rest of her life attempting to subdue her demons. Unfortunately, one of the demons wrote the poems. But she is lucky, as she was so rarely in life, to have this sympathetic biographer, who writes so well, and whose intuitions seem so sound. Louise's exquisite poems are intelligently correlated with the events of her life. I can't imagine anyone reading Frank's book without reaching to the shelf where Louise's poems rest, as I did, or rushing out to buy them. Thanks to the Ecco Press, *The Blue Estuaries,* her complete poems, is still obtainable, so that we may drink in lines like:

Goodbye, goodbye!
There was so much to love, I could not love it all;
I could not love it enough.

Some things I overlooked, and some I could not find.
Let the crystal clasp them
When you drink your wine, in autumn.

Maynard Mack's Pope

Is there another writer so many of whose phrases have entered the everyday language of English-speaking people? Well, yes: there is the only genius-collective, who translated the Bible for King James; Shakespeare; Dickens. But generally, when we quote from them, we are at least dimly aware of the source – although for some, Shakespeare is as good as Holy Writ. But Pope! I venture to say that he is often quoted, or garbled, by people who dimly associate the phrase with ancient lore: "Hope springs eternal in the human breast"; "my guide, philosopher and friend"; "when doctors disagree"; "A little learning is a dangerous thing"; "To err is human, to forgive divine"; "Damn with faint praise"; "Fools rush in where angels fear to tread"; "the human form divine"; "a rage to live"; "speed the parting guest"; "The feast of reason and the flow of soul."

I've stuck to one-liners here, although there are couplets and quatrains almost as well known. And yet . . . Who reads Pope these days other than students and scholars and a few eccentrics like me? (If that last sentence should release a spate of letters saying, "I do, I do!" I shall go gratified to my grave.)

Now Maynard Mack has issued his magisterial biography, *Alexander Pope* (Norton, 1985), "long-awaited," a phrase commonly used to describe a work that we few have yearned for. The book should go a long way towards correcting the picture of Pope (1688–1744) that still lingers on after two centuries – that of a mean, malicious, deformed, vindictive little dwarf. To the degree to which this is believed, Pope's enemies – and they were legion – have triumphed. Not by their calumnious words; they have long since vanished down the maw of time. But collectively their vituperations created a miasma which has obstinately clung to Pope's reputation ever since.

However, the cause is more complex than that. Pope was the last of the neoclassical writers, follower of Dryden, heir of Homer, Horace, Virgil – to whom he addressed these lines:

> Oh may some spark of your celestial fire,
> The last, the meanest of your sons inspire
> (That on weak wings, from far, pursues your flights;
> Glows while he reads, but trembles as he writes).

Although not the meanest, Pope was assuredly the last of their sons. Augustan verse ended with him. No one could equal, let alone surpass, his brilliance in his chosen genre, the heroic couplet. And his use of classical rhetorical devices led to their virtual abandonment as well. There was nowhere for his successors to go except somewhere else. Already, Romantic poetry was beginning to stretch its drowsy wings when Pope was dying... And we have been more or less in thrall to Romantic poetry ever since, right up until the death of Dylan Thomas.

Not that Pope didn't have his Romantic-Pastoral period early on, in these lines written, by his reckoning, at age sixteen, in his early version of "Windsor Forest." A shepherd gazes into a little stream:

> The wat'ry Landscape of the pendant Woods,
> And absent Trees that tremble in the Floods;
> In the clear azure Gleam the Flocks are seen,
> And floating Forest paint the Waves with Green.

One readily forgives Maynard Mack's occasional irritating literary mannerisms when one comes across his speculations on the youth who wrote that passage, "when all raptures are made more rapturous by golden intimations of secret powers ripening." "Premonitions... there must have been of presences in earth, air, stream, and in the mind itself. Not Wordsworthian presences in Pope's case... but not the inert rubble of a classical education either: invented perhaps but also discovered; mysteries of the imagination that haunt us still."

But by the time "Windsor Forest" was published in its final form, when Pope was twenty-five, we see Pope's career developing in the pattern of Virgil, the presiding spirit of this work, from pastoral to georgic to epic. Critics have pointed out that Pope is using descriptions of nature as a metaphor for politics – a way of reflecting on history past and present. I am struck by the parallels to classical Chinese poetry: dialectical in structure, it poses nature's harmonious relationships as paradigms for harmony in the state. Pope and Confucius turn out much the same.

But from now on, Pope becomes increasingly concerned with the corruption of the politics of his time, and turns to the use of human figures rather than natural forms as metaphors for social disintegration. Another common and damaging popular fallacy holds that Pope's chief targets were his contemporaries, the sybarites and hangers-on at court, the literary hacks and toadies. Actually, their principal function is to serve as symbols of the corruption of Sir Robert Walpole's administration (Prime Minister from 1721–1742), and the stupidity and Germanic insularity of the horrible Hanovers. One thing we Americans *do* know about is George the Third; and the previous Georges were equally repellent: among other things obstinate, thickheaded, and refusing to learn the language of the country over which they reigned. Pope is especially bitter that Walpole and the Georges have cynically abandoned any pretense of being patrons of arts and letters. (Although one has to hand it to the Hanovers for honoring Handel.) They turned in contempt from writers they couldn't buy. In 1730, they played with the idea of making Stephen Duck – a semi-articulate farm laborer – poet laureate, but then settled on Colley Cibber, poetaster and playwright of sorts (his specialty consisting of mangled versions of classic plays). Cibber makes the dictionaries of quotations with, "Perish the thought!" – his only thought that hasn't perished. But Cibber lives on, immortalized by Pope:

> Round him much Embryo, much Abortion lay,
> Much future Ode, and abdicated Play;
> Nonsense precipitate, like running Lead,
> That slip'd thro' Cracks and Zig-zags of the Head;
> All that on Folly Frenzy could beget,
> Fruits of dull Heat, and Sooterkins* of Wit.
> Next o'er his Books his eyes began to roll,

*SOOTERKIN: an imaginary afterbirth, "applied to literary compositions etc., of a supplementary or imperfect character" (Shorter Oxford Dictionary).

> In pleasing memory of all he stole,
> How here he sipp'd, how there he plunder'd snug
> And suck's all o'er, like an industrious Bug.
> Here lay poor Fletcher's half-eat scenes, and here
> The frippery of crucify'd Moliere;
> There hapless Shakespear. . . .

Poor guileless Cibber wrote to Pope in protest, "What! Am I only to be dull, and dull still, and again, and forever?" Afraid so. Here one can only quote Pope against himself:

> Satire or sense, alas! can Sporus feel
> Who breaks a butterfly upon a wheel?

This description – or evisceration – of Cibber I have just cited is the kind of Pope people think of when they think of Pope. My own favorite Pope combines the satiric with the lyric in a manner not matched by any other poet in English. Again from *The Dunciad*:

> Intrepid then, o'er seas and lands he flew:
> Europe he saw, and Europe saw him too.
> There all thy gifts and graces we display,
> Thou, only thou, directing all our way!
> To where the Seine, obsequious as she runs,
> Pours at great Bourbon's feet her silken sons;
> Or Tiber, now no longer Roman, rolls,
> Vain of Italian Arts, Italian souls:
> To happy Convents, bosom'd deep in vines,
> Where slumber Abbots, purple as their wines . . .

Yum, yum.

But let us not forget that this lovely, sensuous, seemingly effortless verse poured from a tiny body almost continuously racked with pain: the tuberculosis which stunted him, twisted his spine to hunch his back – probably caught from his wet nurse when he was an infant – and which caused his premature death. For the most part he bore his infirmities with good nature. He wrote Martha Blount about one treatment which consisted of applying hot bricks and tiles to his poor body morning and night, "and sure it is very satisfactory to one who loves architecture at his heart, to be built round in his very bed." The Earl of Oxford wrote that Pope in his later years was, "unable to dress or undress himself, or get into bed without help; nor could he stand upright till a kind of stays, made of stiff linen, were laced on him, one of his sides being contracted almost to the backbone. . . ." Eventually, his body was enclosed in "an iron case." A friend saw his warped and shrivelled figure lifted from it when he died, "like a man whom you hang in chains." But still, while living in it, he kept in spirits, and kept up the extraordinary round of social visiting which perhaps distracted him from his woes. In 1744, months before his death, he addressed two titled friends:

> My dear Lords, – Yes, I would see you as long as I can see you . . . If your charity would take up a small Bird that is half dead of the frost, and set a chirping for half an hour, I'll jump into my Cage, and put myself into your hands. . . ."

You see that I too, like Professor Mack, am an apologist for Pope, attempting to put him in the best possible light, wanting to gloss over his fibs, his not-so-scrupulous maneuverings to put himself before the public without seeming to, his long long memory of injuries to his person or reputation. But have a look at the kind of thing that was said of him by his enemies – although one can't bear to contemplate that savage billingsgate for long: " . . . his life is a Corrosive, that eats first on itself, then on other people . . . His Bow, as his Back informs you, is too weak, and his arrows too short and blunt for Execution, therefore he tips them with the native *Arsenic* of his own Malice. What he calls writing is his poisoning Paper and Reader; he lives on Scandal, like a Maggot on Putrefaction, or a Fly on Excrement." – Henley
Or this:

> But how should'st thou by Beauty's Force be moved
> No more for loving made, than to be lov'd?
> It was such equity of righteous Heav'n
> That such a Soul to such a Form was giv'n.
> – Lady Mary Wortley Montague

These crude and cruel attacks on his shape, his politics, his parents and his religion began in his twenties and continued without let until the end of his life, and after. A famous caricature which received the widest possible circulation pictured Pope as a hunch-backed monkey. It would be idle to pretend that this drumfire of vulgar invective did not embitter Pope as his life – "this long disease, my life" – wore to its close. His satiric denunciations became less an indictment of a society and more a vengeance against personal enemies. Perhaps his dear friend Swift sums it up best: "I have observed some Satyrists to use the Publick much at Rate that Pedants do a naughty Boy ready Hors'd for Discipline: First expostulate the Case, then plead the Necessity of the Rod, from great Provocations, and conclude every Period with a Lash." Swift more than anyone understood the workings of Pope's mind and feelings; in some ways they were very like his own. He once confessed to "Stella" that he had written an anonymous lampoon on a great man who had snubbed him: "But say nothing; t'was only a little revenge."

Much of Pope's venom is directed at people who have vanished without a trace, except for his mention of them. Readers who dip into his work grow impatient with lines like these:

> Slander or poison dread from Delia's rage;
> Hard words or hanging, if your judge be Page;
> From furious Sappho scarce a milder fate,
> Pox'd by her love or libell'd by her hate . . .

Who *are* these people – and who cares? (Delia: The Countess Deloraine, governess to the young Princesses, later to be the King's whore, said to have poisoned a rival; Page: a "judicial sadist"; Sappho: Lady Mary Wortley Montague who may have had syphilis but whose prettiness had been ravaged by smallpox.) Many may empathize with Ezra Pound when he said, "Such reading is not even training for writers. It is a specialized form of archaeology."

In his epilogue to *The Dunciad* Pope has an answer: The reader should not be too troubled or anxious if he can't figure out who the victims are, "since when he shall have found them out, he will probably know no more of the Persons than before." As the brilliant Pope scholar, David B. Morris, remarks in his invaluable book, *Alexander Pope, the Genius of Sense* (Harvard University Press, 1984), they "receive an appropriate form of punishment: they almost disappear." In his persona of the pedant, Scriblerus, Pope says they are condemned to face posterity neither truly remembered nor wholly forgotten: "All phantoms!"

Lady Mary is one of the exceptions. She is still a figure in English literary history by virtue of her letters as well as her relations with Pope, upon which Professor Mack through lack of real evidence isn't able to shed much light. It seems clear from Pope's early letters to her that he was infatuated with her. But it's likely that Pope, not content with protestations via the mails, had an emotional confrontation with her, when she mocked him, his hump, his frailty, his fifty-four inches. At any rate, love turned to hate – in a phrase more suited to bad literature than real life.

Pope was "keenly sensuous," as Peter Quennell has said. "Few English poets have written so feelingly of women and 'the woman's world.' He appreciated women, enjoyed their conversation, acquired an intimate knowledge of their thoughts and habits . . . " And further, he had the courage to be a flirt and a tease. In his most scabrous version of Horace's dirtiest satire, Pope is his own engaging self in this account of an attempted seduction:

> But if to Charms more latent you pretend,
> What Lines encompass, and what Works defend!*
> Dangers on Dangers! Obstacles by dozens!
> Spies, Guardians, Guests, old Women, Aunts and Cozens!
> Could you directly to her Person go,
> Stays will obstruct above, and Hoops below,
> And if the Dame says yes, the Dress says no –

Other lines often quoted to prove his mysogyny have, I feel, quite mistaken his tone: "Most women have no characters at all," and "Every

*LINES: loins.

woman is at heart a rake," are surely playful. One can almost hear him "rallying" – to use a nice old-fashioned word – his affectionate friends, the Blount sisters. His true relations with Martha Blount are also ambiguous and obscure. One hopes and wonders: Did ever a kind woman take him in her arms and rock him like a child?

But, as seems probable, women were only his friends (with the possible exception of a few prostitutes of whom he boasted in his youth), their friendship and that of the many distinguished men who surrounded him were the consolations of his life. Pope on his deathbed said, "There is nothing meritorious but Virtue, & Friendship." Professor Morris points out that Pope shared Aristotle's view that, "although affection resembles an emotion, friendship resembles a moral state, implying purpose, choice and knowledge." But, going beyond Aristotle, friendship for Pope offered consolation, sympathy and understanding – so necessary to this vulnerable little person. Pope understandably disclaims this vulnerability to attack in the wonderful Epitaph he wrote for himself:

> Under this Marble, or under this Sill,
> Or under this Turf, or ev'n what they will,
> Whatever an Heir, or a Friend in his stead,
> Or any good creature shall lay o'er my head,
> Lies one who ne'er cared, and still cares not a pin
> What they said, or may say, of the mortal within. . . .

But here I think we must pay heed to Dr. Johnson: "He pretends insensibility to censure and criticism, though it was observed by all who knew him that every pamphlet disturbed his quiet. . . ."

And what friends! Professor Mack provides an alphabetical list, from which I quote: Atterbury, Arbuthnot, Congreve, Gay, Swift, Bathurst, Bolingbroke, Oxford, the Burlingtons, and on and on. "Nature, temper, and habit, from my youth made me have but one strong desire . . . to fix and preserve a few lasting, dependable friendships." Sadly for him, many of his close friends were older than he, and though Pope died in early middle age, most of his friends preceded him. "I am a man of desperate fortunes," Pope wrote in his late forties, "that is, a man whose friends are dead: for I never aimed at any other fortune than in friends."

> Years foll'wing Years, steal something ev'ry day,
> At last they steal us from our selves away;
> In one our Frolicks, one Amusements end,
> In one a Mistress drops, in one a Friend:
> This subtle Thief of Life, this paltry Time,
> What will it leave me, if it snatch my Rhyme?
> If ev'ry Wheel of that unweary'd Mill
> That turn'd ten thousand Verses, now stands still?

Pope died quietly in May of 1744, insisting with his last breath that the only true source of happiness is virtue. As Maynard Mack concludes, "Without virtue, individuals simply disfigure themselves, creating rigid or incoherent parodies of human nature, as we see in the fate of Pope's satirical victims from *The Rape of the Lock* through *The Dunciad*." Virtue, as Pope put it in "An Essay on Man," "the only point where human bliss stands still." In the course of his life, Pope confronted a society in which corruption greatly accelerated, damaging both the individual and the social order. Pope wrote a friend in 1741: "My Mind at present is as dejected as possible, for I love my Country & I love Mankind, and I see a dismal Scene opening for our own and other Nations." Yet he never quite despaired of our fate, believing that with effort and ethical insight we could reverse the downward slide. Pope! thou shouldst be living at this hour.

A Poet's Pope

ONE OF THE GREAT STRENGTHS of the new biography of Pope is that, unlike most academic critics, Maynard Mack understands *how a poet works*. I am not infrequently surprised, in talking with highly intelligent novelists and critics, to see how far they are from comprehending our particular concerns with the craft. In discussing Pope's translation of Statius, the Latin poet who had attracted both Chaucer and Dante (an understandable attraction when one comes on lines like *saeva dies animi*, "the cruel daylight of the mind") Professor Mack notes that "there is a new energy in (Pope's) verbs." The verb: that armature on which the syntax of the poem is wrapped!

Later Mack speaks of, "the gift Pope had always had of charging his lines with sounds and rhythms felt as much upon the tongue and teeth as heard by the ear. . . ." It is wonderful that he understands so well that the writing of poetry is an intensely *physical* act, involving all parts of the body, every orifice, and each of the five senses.

But for a discussion of traits which make Pope particularly important and attractive to a poet like myself, one must turn to David Morris's *Alexander Pope, the Genius of Sense* (Harvard University Press, 1984), for a quote from an earlier work of Maynard Mack: "Pope thinks of human character as a creative achievement, an artistic result, something built out of chaos as God built the world." Morris goes on to say that, "Man may be, as Pope calls him in 'An Essay on Man', a 'Chaos of Thought and Passion, all confus'd', but he still retains the power of self-possession through an intelligent awareness of his condition, through connecting himself with the past by means of memory, and through sharing a charitable concern for the life around him."

Morris says, "Whether in minor epitaphs or in major Horatian epistles, human character is, for Pope, the poet's special subject." It is *the* subject – and for this poet as well.

Again, speaking as a professional poet (Pope himself was the first of the breed to live without official patronage, handouts, or what we now call "grants"), that is, I'm one who lives by the writing of poetry, and its byproducts, not available to Pope in his day, nor to many English poets in this one: poetry readings, writing workshops, and some teaching of poetry. I would point to what Morris has to say about revision. "As a writer whose major work spans three decades, [Pope] was constantly revisiting and revising his own compositions. Revision, in its richest sense, is the characteristic activity of Pope's writing. Homer, Virgil, Lucretius, Horace . . . all are in various ways 'revised' by Pope as he appropriates their virtues for his work . . . Revision for Pope is a great deal more than a technique of composition. It is a mode of thought, a natural rhythm, a way of life." In a letter, Pope said, of translating Homer: "I correct daily, and make (the verses) seem less corrected, that is, more easy, more fluent, more natural."

Pope was quite aware, as most working poets are, that the lines which seem to the reader or critic most spontaneous, graceful and natural are often the ones laboriously revised, far into the night, with an obbligato of curses and an outpouring of sweat. When Pope was praised for his powers of fancy and imaginative vision, he chose to emphasize the process of revision, once calling it, "the greatest proof of judgment of anything I ever did." With practice, revision itself becomes a creative act, not simply drudgery, but accompanied by the same excitement with which one sets down a first draft. One learns dispassion, judgment, and a certain limited faith in one's own powers of discrimination. Of course there are many poets, from Byron to the present (I could name names but I won't) who accept the Romantic notion that equates spontaneity with poetic genius. Pope, by contrast, locates revising at the heart of the poetic process.

Pope maintained that he always waited at least two years before publishing. As this is a habit of my own, I applaud it! (Although there are always exceptions, particularly with minor pieces that are tossed off, prompted by some occasion or other.) In "An Epistle to Dr. Arbuthnot," Pope advises lesser poets to, "Keep your Piece nine years" (something I've done at least three times in my life, with pieces that seemed important to me). But of course it's the very people who ought to do this who feel the need to hustle into print, lest they be forgotten. They will be, needless to say, but I suppose the hope is that they will last their own lifetimes.

It would be fruitless to try to label the man as, "Pope, our Contemporary" as Jan Kott labelled "Shakespeare, our Contemporary." Despite valiant efforts to convince us of Pope's relevance in every department of modern life, Professor Mack fails to convince very many of us. Pope, of all poets, is a man of his time. But that doesn't mean that there aren't a few of us who deeply value Greek and Roman poetry (I've been called "Roman" by at least two serious critics – not bad for someone who doesn't know Latin – but then we're informed that Pope's Latin wasn't adequate), who love Pope: the wit, the skill, the syntax, yes, the man. It's good to feel part of a line that stretches back so far, to Homer, to Sappho. My aim is to strive to be, as Pope was, a worthy link.

The Green Man: John Clare

JOHN CLARE, THE MARVELOUS English naturalist-poet whose bicentennial occurs in 1993, is still largely unknown, except perhaps to readers who have come across his great poem, "I Am" in an anthology of English poetry. And in collections for children, Clare's "Little Trotty Wagtail" can sometimes be found. To this day there is no American edition of Clare's poetry. I first heard the name of John Clare in the mid-fifties when Theodore Roethke recited "The Badger" to his poetry class in the deep, gravelly dramatic voice I still hear when I read the poem. Others in the class beside myself, including the late James Wright, fell in love with Clare's poem: the extraordinary plosive force in the lines, the hammering of the monosyllables, the naked verbs at the end:

> He falls as dead and kicked by boys and men
> Then starts and grins and drives the crowd agen
> Till kicked and torn and beaten out he lies
> And leaves his hold and cackles groans and dies.

Then for some of us the hunt was on: bedevilling librarians for books they did not have, searching second-hand bookstores for English editions of his poetry, editions, we did not realize at that time, seriously flawed by the emendations of conventional editors. Alterations of spelling and grammar, and even censorship of Clare's "radical" ideas, began with his first manuscript, published in 1820, and continued until the mid-sixties of this century. But I was grateful to come upon a copy of *John Clare: Poems Chiefly from Manuscript* (G. P. Putnam's Sons, 1921), edited by Edmund Blunden and Alan Porter, which had been published in 1920. Later I was able to obtain *Selected Poems of John Clare* (Dutton, 1965), edited by Geoffrey Grigson in 1950, then James Reeves's selection, published in 1954, and later still I acquired Grigson's *Poems of John Clare's Madness* (Routledge and K. Paul, 1949), which had been published in 1949, with vast numbers of poems not found in the other books.

The frustrating part of studying these volumes was that a favorite poem from one was usually missing from the others. For example, in his 1920 edition, Grigson includes the wonderful sonnet, "The Mouse's Nest," but one searches for it in vain in Blunden or Reeves:

> I found a ball of grass among the hay
> And progged it as I past and went away
> And when I looked I fancied something stirred
> And turned agen and hoped to catch the bird –
> When out an old mouse bolted in the wheats
> With all her young ones hanging at her teats
> She looked so odd and so grotesque to me
> I ran and wondered what the thing could be
> And pushed the knapweed bushes where I stood
> Then the mouse hurried from the craking brood
> The young ones squeaked and as I went away
> She found her nest agen among the hay
> The water oer the pebbles scarce could run
> And broad old cesspools glittered in the sun

Perhaps Blunden and Reeves considered "teats" and "cesspools" vulgar. (How much more shocking, then, if they had known that in the original manuscript Clare wrote "sex-pools" – from a personal letter of Eric Robinson.)

A poem called "Summer" in Reeves begins, "How sweet, when weary, dropping on a bank..." while in Grigson a poem called "Summer" begins, "The Oak's slow-opening leaf, of deepening hue..." while Blunden has no "Summer" whatsoever.

The two-volume edition of Clare's poems edited by J. W. Tibble and his wife Anne, published in 1935 and finally obtained at a rare book dealer's, assuaged some frustrations and supplied others. Like the other editors, the Tibbles added punctuation, selectively cleaned up Clare's erratic spelling, altered colloquial words to conform to conventional usage, and omitted important poems without any discernable reason for doing so. The Tibbles's Clare was a largely asexual being, with few observable opinions on anything that might be construed as politically radical or theologically unorthodox. Still, it should be remembered that it was the Tibbles who introduced Clare – or rather reintroduced him, after the lapse of a century – to British readers, although the full measure of his genius came to be realized only in the mid-sixties: Eric Robinson and Geoffrey Summerfield's *The Later Poems of John Clare* contained faithful and accurate texts of the poems. Their editing of *The Shepherd's Calendar,* published the same year, was the first authentic and uncut text of this vivid parade of the seasons in Clare's Northamptonshire countryside.[1]

Two years later, Robinson and Summerfield published *Clare: Selected Poems and Prose* (Oxford University Press, 1966) and standards were firmly established: fidelity to Clare's dialect form of words, his spelling, his lack of punctuation or occasional over-punctuation – standards which have been largely observed by subsequent editors. Another decade elapsed before serious critical attention began to be paid to Clare, and the landscape and the social environment from which he sprang. Now, in the seventies and eighties, one could begin to piece together an accurate outline of Clare's life. Some gifted Marxist critics, notably John Barrell and Raymond Williams, were attracted to the figure of Clare as an exemplar of the articulate laborer in the rural society of the eighteenth century, oppressed by landowners, hired at starvation wages, and deprived, by the infamous Acts of Enclosure, of traditional rights going back to the thirteenth century.

Yet Clare is still the most neglected major poet in our language. He was cursed with bad luck from the start. The first of his misfortunes was that he was born in 1793, five years after Byron, a year later than Shelley, and two years before Keats. (He outlived them all by many years and continued to write until the time of Tennyson and Browning, and died a year before the birth of Yeats.) Born earlier or later he might not have been cast so firmly in the shadow of these superstars.

[1]Manchester, 1964

There was a brief flare of fame when his first book was published, and then he sank into the obscurity which persisted until our own time.

Initially, what intrigued the British public was that Clare was published and publicized as "The Peasant Poet," and treated with the condescension accorded Robert Bloomfield and Stephen Duck, though Clare was no peasant but a landless laborer like his father. Clare contributed to this false stereotype by self-deprecating references to his poems as "the unpolished heartfelt feelings of a lowly Clown (a rustic) who is not acquainted with the craft and Subtlety of Art to make them agreable to the tasteful Eye."

In truth, Clare was exceptionally well-read. He read everything he could get his hands on, from *Little Red Riding Hood* to *Pilgrim's Progress;* he read and re-read the prophetical books of the Bible; he owned books on land-surveying, botany, philosophy, astrology and herbal medicine. In poetry, Thompson's *The Seasons* was the first book he ever bought, with painfully saved pennies, and was the first important and continuing influence on his work. Clare knew the sonnets of Shakespeare, Milton, Dryden and Surrey. He esteemed Pope at a time when that poet was out of fashion (a taste he shared with Byron); he was interested in Donne, who was in virtual eclipse then and for a century to come. He was familiar with Chaucer and Marvell.

In a letter to his publishers, October 1824, he wrote: "I never take up Johnson's *Lives* but I regret his beginning at the wrong end first and leaving out those beautiful minstrels of Elizabeth – had he forgot that there had been such poets as Spencer, Drayton, Suckling? But it was the booksellers' judgement that employed his pen and we know by experience most of their judgements lye in their pockets; so the poets of Elizabeth are still left in cobwebs and mystery." So speaks one "not acquainted with the craft and Subtlety of Art."

But the worst curse laid on Clare was unremitting poverty and hard labor in the fields, fens and quarries. In 1820 Thomas Hood described him: "There was a slightness about his frame, with a delicacy of feature and complexion, that associated him more with the Garden than with the Field... There was much about Clare for a Quaker to like; he was tender-hearted and averse to violence..."[2] Even at the height of his

[2]Thomas Hood (Prose Works)

fame when his first book sold 4,000 copies in the first year (while Keats and Shelley sold barely 500 copies each) his publishers paid him almost nothing, and he was forced to continue working as a common laborer. This work, and the unceasing anxiety he felt about keeping his parents, his wife, and seven children from actual starvation, undoubtedly contributed to the mental illness which confined him to insane asylums for more than a quarter of a century, until his long life ended.

Clare was born in the village of Helpston in Northamptonshire, which consisted of little more than a single street lined with cottages, taverns and a church. The fens lay to the north and east, causing everyone nearby to suffer from "fen ague," a type of malaria for which the standard specifics were opium and brandy. Clare was always prone to fen ague, and perhaps to the remedies as well, until he was put away.

> So moping flat and low our valleys lie
> So dull and muggy is our winter sky
> Drizzling from day to day dull threats of rain
> And when that falls still threatening on again
> From one wet week so great an ocean flows
> That every village to an island grows
> And every road for even weeks to come
> Is stopt and none but horsemen go from home . . .
>
> (from "Winter in the Fens")

To the west and south of the village was a landscape with "a wealth of wild-flowers, woodlands, heaths and gentle valleys" where "the birds were song-birds rather than the coarse-voiced creatures of marsh and flood," as Edward Storey describes it in his life of Clare.[3]

He was the eldest child of Parker and Anne Clare (his twin, a girl, died a few weeks later). His illiterate mother early sensed her child's unusual gifts, and was eager for him to have as much education as the family could manage, in hopes that he could rise above the level of a laborer in the fields. (Cambridge, only a few miles away, might as well have been on the moon.) Clare went to a Dame's school in Helpston, for three months out of the year at most, for even little children were

[3]*A Right to Song: The Life of John Clare* (Methuen, 1982)

needed for tasks at home. Later, his mother claimed to Octavius Gilchrist, a friend of Clare's, that her son could read a chapter of the Bible before he was six.

Then Clare attended a village school in Glinton, two miles away, where the master was impressed with his reading and his remarkable memory. There he met a little girl named Mary Joyce, the daughter of a prosperous farmer. Mary was about eight when they met, Clare four years older. They parted in their teens, perhaps owing to the opposition of her parents, perhaps because Mary felt above him socially, or perhaps only because of Clare's shyness and reticence. But Clare never forgot her. Though he was to take a casual or romantic interest in many women, Mary was his muse for the rest of his life. The dozens upon dozens of poems he wrote to her – or, in the days of his madness, wrote to other women with Mary in mind – attest to his never-fading adoration, though these poems are widely varying in quality.

> I was a lover very early in life, my first attachment being a schoolboy affection, but Mary, who cost me more ballads than sighs, was beloved with a romantic or Platonic sort of feeling . . . our talk was of play, and our actions the wanton nonsense of children. Yet young as my heart was it would turn chill when I touched her hand, and tremble, and I fancyed her feelings were the same; for as I gazed earnestly in her face, a tear would hang in her smiling eye and she would turn and wipe it away. Her heart was as tender as a bird's+

Clare's formal education ended when he was thirteen so that he could hire out as a laborer like the other village boys, although at his teacher's urging, he attended night school for a time. But his poet's education was not confined to book learning at school and book reading at home. His parents amused themselves in the evenings by singing the old folk ballads like "Barbara Allen" and "Lord Randal." Both parents were admired locally as tellers of tales; his father was a popular entertainer at village festivities, and boasted that he knew above a hundred traditional songs by heart.

A crone named Granny Bains taught him more ballads and narrative

---

+Eric Robinson and Geoffrey Summerfield, eds. *Clare: Selected Poems and Prose* (Oxford University Press, 1966 and 1967)

verses while he was tending sheep or scaring off crows. Clare loved to haunt the camp of the gypsies – "a quiet, pilfering, unprotected race" he was to write – to listen to their fiddles and learn their songs. One critic has said that the gypsies "had a strange fascination for Clare." Not so strange. While Clare and his kind joined "catchwork gangs," worked as ploughboys, lime-burners, gardeners – at all hours, in all weathers – the gypsies were free.

Clare's songs were "born in music" in the words of Eric Robinson, "in the scrape of the fiddle and in the voices of his mother and father singing in that small cottage in Helpston." By his early teens he was composing ballads and rhymes in imitation of the models he had learned. He tried them out on his parents who could see little merit in them and laughed, until Clare pretended that he had copied them from a book. Then they approved.

Finding suitable surfaces on which to write was a problem then, and for the rest of his life. At that time he used bits of bills on blue paper and brown wrapping paper from the grocer, and hid the poems in a hole in the wall. His mother, thinking that he was just practicing his handwriting, often used them as squibs for lighting the fire.

In his poems a characteristic beat was the steady rhythm of his mother's spinning wheel: "I measured this ballad today wi the thrumming of my mother's wheel if it be tinctured wi the drone of that domestic music you will excuse it after this confession," Clare wrote to his publishers in May 1820. In the final stanza of "Clifford Hill" one hears the ground rhythm of the poem, the click of the shuttle and the click-clack of the mill:

> Yes dearly do these scenes I love
> And dear that fir clad hill
> There all secure does build the dove
> While click-clack goes the mill
> And now in natures sweet repose
> I leave this spot awile
> The bee is buried in the rose
> And man gone from his toil

Surely the click-clack is also the ticking of a clock which expresses the passing of time as does the flow of water over the mill wheel. The busy activity of the first lines gives way to a more langourous measure, and its "sweet repose" and the bee "buried" in the rose hint at a final rest, just as the man gone from his toil may be gone forever. This stanza conveys so much that one must feel that only the rigidities of the English class system could lead some early critics to treat Clare as little better than a simpleton.

Early on, Clare tackled a great variety of forms. In addition to ballads he tried terza rima, rhymed couplets, and increasingly, as time went on, sonnets in rhymed couplets, as well as sonnets which separated the octave and the sestet, and some with a single unified movement, "overflowing" as Wordsworth put it, "into the second portion of the metre." Instead of looking at the sonnet as a piece of architecture, "I have been much in the habit of preferring the image of an orbicular body – a sphere – or a dew drop."[5] Clare too came to prefer this style in the course of writing hundreds of sonnets.

Clare liked to refer to "a dancing measure" which grew from the rhythm of the fiddle, the gypsy music, the ballad meters, and perhaps the sound of his own footsteps on the turf as he wandered the countryside. In another letter to his publisher, February 28, 1823, he wrote: "I have got into this dancing measure which runs so easy that I can hardly get out of it . . ." And he never did.

One of his rampageous dancing ballads must have delighted Theodore Roethke. "My Last Shilling," from Clare's first book, begins:

> O dismal disaster! O troublesome lot!
> What a heart rending theme for my musing Ive got
> Then pray whats the matter? O friend Im not willing
>   The thought grieves me sore
>   Now Im drove to the shore
> And must I then spend the last shilling, the shilling
> And must I then spend the last shilling?

"Mouse-poor," in Robert Graves' tender description, Clare was a proud lad, and until the end, after unspeakable adversities, a proud man. Diminutive though he was, he could stand up to bullies, and was

---

[5]Wordsworth, letter to Alexander Dyer, 1833

capable of turning from his door the prying strangers with their inso-
lent queries who descended on him after his successful first book. In his
poetry, though, this pride combined with a characteristic modesty,
as in these lines from "The Progress of Rhyme" (Clare spelled it
"Ryhme"), written in early days:

> I felt that I'd a right to song
> And sung—but in a timid strain
> Of fondness for my native plain
> For everything I felt a love
> The weeds below the birds above
> And weeds that blossomed in summers hours
> I thought they should be reckoned flowers...

> And so it cheered me while I lay
> Among their beautiful array
> To think that I in humble dress
> Might have a right to happiness
> And sing as well as greater men
> And then I struck the lyre agen...

Meanwhile he helped his father who was growing increasingly crippled
by rheumatism. He worked as a ploughboy, and at one period he was
hired by the proprietor of The Blue Bell, a tavern next to his cottage,
where he worked for nearly a year, and where he learned to drink. His
fits and starts of employment went on for years, but to detail them con-
tributes little to understanding his development as a poet. His true oc-
cupation was to wander in the fields and woodland, lying silent in the
grass for hours at a time, inspecting the busy insects, admiring the
weeds, or keeping watch over a bird's nest, carefully noting the color
and number of its eggs, and awaiting the parent bird's return. These are
the themes in poems that contemporary poets who are fortunate
enough to know Clare's work, love the best. An early poem like "The
Lark's Nest" displays his careful eye for detail as well as the freshness
and immediacy of his vision:

> From yon black clump of wheat that grows
> More rank and higher than the rest

A lark—I marked her as she rose—
   At early morning left her nest.
Her eggs were four of dusky hue
   Blotched brown as is the very ground
With tinges of a purply hue
   The larger ends encircling round.

Behind a clod how snug the nest
   Is in a horses footing fixed
Of twitch and stubble roughly dressed
   With roots and horsehair intermixed.
The wheat surrounds it like a bower
   And like to thatch each bowing blade
Throws off the frequent falling shower
   —And heres an egg this morning laid!

Clare's way of seeing and writing presaged a shift in sensibility which was not appreciated by his critics and fellow poets, who felt that Nature should be only a vehicle for expressing a philosophic thought or an abstract idea, and did not consist in praising weeds. Early commentators complained that his poems were not poetry but leaves from a naturalist's notebook.

Clare composed hastily, but this was caused by his compelling need to catch the experience in words even as it was unfolding for him. The specificity of his descriptions, their particularity, was an intrinsic part of his capture of immediate reality. (One of the reasons he fought to retain his dialect words was that they conveyed his exact meaning; no word in the conventional literary vocabulary would do.) As William Howard points out in his *John Clare* (Twayne, 1981), Clare composed his poems "during or immediately after the rapturous experience itself." Among hundreds of examples here is a sonnet which Clare seems to be composing as he walks along, "Sudden Shower":

Black grows the southern sky betokening rain
   And humming hive-bees homeward hurry by
They feel the change so let us shun the grain
   And take the broad road while our feet are dry
Aye there some dropples moistened on my face

And pattered on my hat—tis coming nigh!
Lets look about and find a sheltering place
    The little things around like you and I
Are hurrying through the grass to shun the shower
    Here stoops an ash tree—hark! the wind gets high
But never mind, this ivy for an hour
    Rain as it may will keep us dryly here
That little wren knows well his sheltering bower
    Nor leaves his dry house though we come so near.

One pictures Clare tucking a rain-spotted scrap of paper into his hat as he sheltered in the bower with the wren.

Unsophisticated though he seemed when during four brief visits he penetrated London literary circles, with his funny grass-green coat and the comportment of a bumpkin, Clare was a knowing writer, a modern in a way that none of the rest of them were, with a sturdy trust in his own way of writing. Charles Lamb would urge him to abandon natural speech and provincial phrasing: "I think you are too profuse with them. There is a rustick Cockneyism as little pleasing as ours of London. Transplant Arcadia to Helpstone . . ." Clare didn't.

John Taylor, publisher of both Keats and Clare, advised him that "your Poetry is much the best when you are not describing common things, and if you would raise your views generally, & speak of the Appearances of Nature . . . more philosophically (if I may say so) or with more Excitement, you would greatly improve these little poems." Clare wouldn't.

Earlier, Taylor had written him that he thought that Keats "wishes to say to you that your Images from Nature are too much introduced without being called for by a particular Sentiment . . ." Clare was not about to take this lying down. Keats, he wrote, "keeps up a constant alusion or illusion to the Grecian mythology & there I cannot follow . . . the frequency of such classical accompaniments make it wearisome to the reader where behind every rose bush he looks for a Venus & under every laurel a thrumming Appollo . . ." Rather than using Nature to illustrate ideas or philosophic concepts, Clare preferred to have Nature use *him*—to be the vessel through which the beauties and bounties of Nature would be poured out for all the world to know.

"No ideas but in things!" – as long as those "things" sang, squeaked, blossomed, nested, soared or loved – would have been a credo quite acceptable to Clare. One of his editors defined Clare's style as composed of "frugality of epithet, vigor, and originality of verbs." Verbs! – the poem's armature around which all else is molded. This emphasis on verbs is characteristic of the Metaphysical poets, but not of the other poets of Clare's day. Clare's verbs were not only original, they were active, potent, brusque or clipped; unlike his peers, he relied heavily on monosyllables. His poems signal the shift away from the noun and the overuse of adjectives back to the verb, an important reason for his appeal to the modern sensibility. Clare had learned from "the poets of Elizabeth" that he loved, as Theodore Roethke and those he taught learned from the Metaphysicals and from Clare himself.

Roethke's line, "I'm odd and full of love" is even more descriptive of Clare than of its author. Though the world of Nature was Clare's constant theme, he lived equally in a world of love.

> I love to see the old heath's withered break
> Mingle its crimpled leaves with furze and ling
> While the old heron from the lonely lake
> Starts slow and flaps his melancholy wing
> And oddling crow in idle motions swing
> On the half rotten ash trees topmost twig...
>
> (from "Emmonsail's Heath in Winter")

Poem after poem contains the phrase, "I love to see" or "I love to hear"; poems begin with lines such as "I love thy shade / Wild arbour on the rude heath growing," or "I love in summertime to seek a seat / Wading the long grass where a path neer led / Patting their downy tops with idle feet," or "I love to drop in summer on the grass / & with unwearied eye mark pleasing things," or "I love to peep out on a summers morn / Just as the scouting rabbit seeks her shed," or "I love to roam in spring by hedgerow sides / These old enclosures mossed by many years..." But there is a significant variation: "I love thee sweet Mary but love thee in fear..."

Mary, whose sensitive response to Nature chimed so harmoniously with his own, was becoming the single figure in his mental landscape, the half of him that made him whole.

> We loved and in each others power Felt nothing to condemn
> I was the leaf and she the flower And both grew on one stem.
>
> (from "The Sweetest Woman There")

Stanzas from "First Love" contain the clearest expression of Clare's predicament: words that he could whisper to himself but could not manage to speak to Mary:

> No single hour can pass for naught
>   No moment-hand can move
> But calendars an aching thought
>   Of my first lonely love
>
> Where silence doth the loudest call
>   My secret to betray
> As moonlight holds the night in thrall
>   As sun reveals the day
>
> I hide it in the silent shades
>   Till silence finds a tongue
> I mark its grave where time invades
>   Till time becomes a song . . .
>
> When words refuse before a crowd
>   My Marys name to give
> The muse in silence sings aloud
>   And there my love will live.

(It might be worth noting that Clare's casual use of nouns for verbs, as in "calendars," was frowned on in his day, though now it has become a commonplace.)

But the mental and spiritual landscape which Clare and Mary shared, that landscape within walking distance in every direction from the fourteenth century cross in the center of Helpston, was undergoing change. Even before Clare was born and as he was gaining manhood the Enclosure Acts of Parliament were depriving laborers and cottagers of their ancient traditional rights. By nearly four thousand acts since the second quarter of the eighteenth century, more than six million acres of land were appropriated through the political influence of the great lords and other wealthy landowners: this was one-fourth of all cultivated acreage which was removed from common use and absorbed into the estates of the wealthy. Janet Todd has said "the enclosing of the land, segmenting the open moorland, physically altered the environment of the peasants. Field work, neither as communal nor as open as before, became more monotonous; cultivators turned into hired laborers; and the link between work and enjoyment, as expressed in the village rites that had once been a part of rural life, was broken."[6]

> Then came enclosure – ruin was her guide
> But freedom's clapping hands enjoyed the sight
> Tho comforts cottage soon was thrust aside
> And workhouse prisons raised upon the site
> Een natures dwelling far away from men
> The common heath became the spoilers prey
> The rabbit had not where to make his den
> And labours only cow was drove away
> No matter – wrong was right and right was wrong
> And freedoms brawl was sanction to the song . . .

(from "To a Fallen Elm")

(This is a rare example of savage irony in Clare's poetry; his social protest more commonly took the mood of grief and indignation.) The loss of freedom to which Clare ironically refers includes the loss of common rights such as the laborers' ability to collect firewood on heath-land. Eric Robinson says that "Clare saw venerable trees cut down, whole coppices destroyed, and the streams diverted from their natural courses. The commons were fenced off, and 'No Trespassing' notices posted. Old women were forbidden to gather sticks from the hedges, and laborers were transported for taking a hare for the pot." In a fur-

[6]Janet Todd, *In Adam's Garden: a study of John Clare's pre-asylum poetry* (University of Florida Press, 1973)

ther irony, not lost on Clare, not only did the laborer lose access to the land, but he was forced, in the words of Raymond Williams, "to do the actual work of draining, levelling and fencing the old landscape" now denied him.

> But sweating slaves I do not blame
>   Those slaves by wealth decreed
> No I should hurt their harmless name
>   To brand 'em wi' the deed
> Although their aching hands did wield
>   The axe that gave the blow
> Yet twas not them that own'd the field
>   Nor planned its overthrow . . .

(from "The Lamentation of Round-Oak Waters")

Williams, the author of *The Country and the City* (Chatto and Windus, 1973)—an invaluable book, along with John Barrell's *An Idea of Landscape and a Sense of Place in the Poetry of John Clare* (Cambridge University Press, 1972), which relates English literature to its social background—has said that if this poem had been printed in full, Clare would have been labelled a radical. But, savagely critical though he was of the ways in which the powerful damaged the weak, and reduced the laborer to a condition little better than serfhood, Clare was profoundly conservative in the old true sense before the term became corrupted by modern politicians. His deepest desire was to have the ways of Nature and the ancient tracks of man and beast remain as they had always been.

In the winter of 1821, the owner of Clare's cottage was threatening to chop down two ancient elms. Clare wrote to his publisher:

My two favorite elm trees at the back of the hut are condemned to die—it shocks me to relate but tis true. The savage who owns them thinks they have done their best and now he wants to make use of the benefits he can get from selling them. O was this country Egypt and I was but a Caliph the owner should lose his ears for his arrogant presumption and the first wretch that buried his axe in their roots should hang on their branches . . . Yet this mourning over trees is all foolishness . . . a second thought tells me I am a fool; were people all to feel as I do the world could not be carried on—a green would not be ploughed up—a tree or bush would not be cut for firing or furniture, and everything they found when boys would remain in that state until they died . . ."

But later, when Taylor, his publisher, asked a mutual friend, Octavius Gilchrist, to intervene, Clare had third thoughts: "Let them die like the rest of us."

John Taylor was a bookseller. Clare's attempt to find someone to print his work had met with repeated rebuffs and frustrations. Finally, in 1819, he showed his manuscript to a Stamford bookseller named Drury, who sent it to Taylor, his cousin. Taylor and his partner, Hessey, were interested, and after considerable editing of Clare's spelling, and the excising of passages thought to offend the delicate-minded public, they published *Poems Descriptive of Rural Life and Scenery* in 1820, which caused a mild sensation.

Taylor was a complex and curious character: evasive, particularly about money, procrastinating, easily distracted and progressively less concerned with poetry, for which he had once had a genuine feeling. But the public was becoming less interested in "peasant poets," indeed in poetry in general, and increasingly turned towards the novel. Taylor ended up as a textbook publisher. However, in his Introduction to *Poems Descriptive* he made some shrewd comments designed to protect Clare's language from the sneers of the learned. He took up Clare's habit of making verbs from substantives, as in the lines "Dark and darker glooms the sky" or "Spring's pencil pinks thee in thy flushy stain." "But in this he has done no more than the man who first employed 'crimson' as a verb . . . But a very great number of those words which are generally called new are, in fact, some of the oldest in our language: many of them are extant in the works of our earliest authors; and a still greater number float on the popular voice . . . Many of the provincial expressions to which Clare has been forced to have recourse, are of this description, forming a large number of what may be called the unwritten language of England."

Clare's assessment of Taylor, though caustic, is remarkably fair, if one considers the increasing indifference with which he treated his poet: "Taylor is a man of very pleasant address and works himself into the good opinions of people in a moment but it is not lasting for he grows into a studied carelessness and neglect . . . he professed a great friendship for me at my first starting and offered to correct my future poems if he did not publish them so I sent all my things up as I wrote them and neither got his opinion or the poems back again his only opinion being that he had not time to spare from other pursuits . . ."[7] To read Clare's letters to Taylor over the years calls up the image of a man beating with bruised knuckles on a locked and bolted door.

But first Clare had his little fame. In London he was entertained by Taylor's acquaintances, among them Lamb, George Darley, H. F. Carey (the translator of Dante), Hazlett, Coleridge and DeQuincy. (Clare's assessment of these gentlemen makes amusing reading. His descriptions, and estimations of their character were perceptive and acute and rarely unkind, only so when their condescensions and suggestions for his improvement were unwelcome.) For his initial visit to London Clare appeared in the coat of grass-green which caused comment. Thomas Hood wrote that the coat was "shining verdantly out from the grave-coloured suits of the literati," some of whom remarked on the coat's appropriate symbolism, and dubbed Clare "the green man."

Only two months after the publication of *Poems Descriptive*, Clare married Patty Turner who was seven months pregnant. Like Blake, he married an illiterate woman who signed the marriage certificate with a shaky "X." Their daughter, Anne Maria, was born on June 2, 1820:

> & much I wish what ere may be
> The lot my child which falls to thee
> Nature neer may let thee see
>   Her glass betimes
> But keep thee from my failings free
>   Nor itch at rhymes . . .
>
> May thou unknown to rhyming bother
> Be ignorant as is thy mother
> & in thy manners such another

[7]Robinson and Summerfield, *Clare: Selected Poems and Prose* (Oxford University Press, 1966 & 1967)

Save sins nigh guest
And then wi scaping this & tother
Thou mayst be blest...

(from "To An Infant Daughter")

These stanzas may reveal Clare's ambivalence about Patty, ignorant and gentle, and also about himself. That "glass," as well as a mirror of nature is associated with "failings" in the following line, and could refer consciously or otherwise to Clare's drinking, which was becoming a problem.

It's no wonder that he increasingly sought refuge with his rough companions at the Blue Bell. Child followed child in rapid succession, and he had his parents and sister to support as well. He worried constantly as to how he would feed them, and compared his situation to that of Bloomfield, who "had not a hundred pounds a year to maintain five or six in the family why I have not fifty pounds to maintain eight with This is a hungry difference."[8]

But Clare also derived comfort and companionship of a higher order. Upon the publication of his book, Clare was invited by Lord Milton to come to Milton Hall and bring ten copies of his book. After being tendered a meal in the servant's hall which he was too nervous to eat or drink, Clare was ushered into his lordship's presence, along with the Fourth Earl Fitzwilliam, and his wife. On leaving, Clare was offered the largest sum of money he had ever seen, seventeen pounds. But it goes without saying that these gentry were not to be friends but intermittent patrons. A pity that the barriers of class were so unbreachable, because Milton was a modest and accomplished naturalist. But no, it was the friendship of Earl Fitzwilliam's butler and head gardener that was to brighten his life. It is difficult for an American to comprehend a class system where the butler of a minor lord could be a distinguished archaeologist, and his head gardener an accomplished botanist. The only parallel which comes to mind is with the once-renowned Prince Esterhazy, now known to us as the man who treated the great

---

[8] J. W. and Anne Tibble, eds. *The Prose of John Clare* (Routlege & Kegan Paul, London, 1951)

composer Haydn as one of the hired help.

Because Clare preferred "the vulgar names to the flowers...as I know no others," (letter to Hessey) some critics, including Barrell, assume that this was true, and not another instance of Clare's self-deprecation. But Joseph Henderson, the gardener-botanist, had read Linnaeus, Gilbert White, and Erasmus Darwin, and possessed an extensive library of books on natural philosophy, *The Florist's Directory,* and *The Culture and Management of the Auricula, Polyanthus, Carnation, Pink and the Ranunculus.*

The butler, Edmund Tyrell Artis, was the author of *Antediluvian Phytology* and *The Durobrivae of Antoninus,* rare and valuable books. Clare wrote that Henderson and Artis were "well-informed men not unacquainted with books & I never met with a party of more happy and heartier fellows in my life there was Artis up to the neck in the old Roman coins & broken pots of the Romans and Henderson never wearied with hunting after the Emperor butterfly & the hornet sphinx in the Hanglands Wood and the orchises on the Heath."[9]

In a letter to Taylor in 1822, Clare said that Artis "has discovered a multitude of fresh things & a fine roman bath is one of the latest discoverys the painted plaster on the walls was very fresh & fine when I saw it & the flues of the furnaces was a proof without the least supposition of its being a bath he has also found the roman road that led to the river & the pavement is as fine as when first laid down...his plan of the Roman City is nearly compleated..."[10] One is grateful for these moments of intense pleasure which Clare derived from their company, the stimulation to his imagination, to his sense of the past as a living presence.

An entry in his Journal for twenty-six December, 1824, reads in part, "I never walk on this bank but the legions of the roman army pass bye my fancy with their mysterys of the 2000 years hanging like a mist around them..."[11] Although his descriptive powers can bring the past to vivid life, Clare's deep belief was that Nature was immortal, not man or his works:

[9]J. W. and Anne Tibble, eds. *The Letters of John Clare* (Routledge & Kegan Paul, 1951)
[10]*Letters*
[11]Margaret Grainger, ed. *The Natural History Prose Writings of John Clare* (Oxford, 1983)

Leaves from eternity are simple things
To the world's gaze where to a spirit clings
Sublime and lasting – trampled underfoot
The daisy lives and strikes its little root
Into the lap of time – centurys may come
And pass away into the silent tomb
And still the child hid in the womb of time
Shall smile and pluck them when this simple rhyme
Shall be forgotten like a church yard stone
Or lingering lye unnotised and alone . . .

(from "The Eternity of Nature")

Consider the tenth and eleventh stanzas of "The Flitting":

Some sing the pomps of chivalry
    As legends of the ancient time
Where gold and pearls and mystery
    Are shadows painted for sublime
But passions of sublimity
    Belong to plain and simpler things
And David underneath a tree
    Sought when a shepherd Salems springs

Where moss did into cushions spring
    Forming a seat of velvet hue
A small unnoticed trifling thing
    To all but heavens hailing dew
And David's crown hath passed away
    Yet poesy breathes his shepherd-skill
His palace lost – and to this day
    The little moss is blooming still . . .

And the final stanza:

Time looks on pomp with vengeful mood
    Or killing apathy's disdain
So where old marble cities stood
    Poor persecuted weeds remain
She feels a love for little things

> That very few can feel beside
> And still the grass eternal springs
> Where castles stood and grandeur died.

(One of Clare's most significant poems – only published three-quarters of a century after he wrote it.) Time "feels a love for little things..." So did Clare. Nothing in Nature was insignificant to him. In a thoughtful essay, Naomi Lewis remarked that unlike other writers of his time, "he did not perceive the unremarkable local scene in vistas but in miniature detail. As Dickens saw people, Clare seems always to have viewed his rural world from a child's level, each object slightly more insistent than in life." (Like Keats, Clare was only five feet tall.) "A flat Northampton field would thus be a paradise of little plants, fragile insects, snail shells, grasses, weeds, 'the heaving grasshopper in his delicate green bouncing from stub to stub' or overhead 'the wild geese skudding along and making all the letters of the alphabet as they flew.'"[12]

After protracted negotiations and pressing letters from Clare, *The Village Minstrel* was published in two volumes late in 1821. The book sold a respectable 800 copies, but the critics' interest had cooled. "Peasant poets" were now out of fashion. And as usual, Clare was paid almost nothing by his negligent or callous publisher.[13] In addition, the Tibbles tell us in their life of Clare, he had to put up with Taylor's "wincing, spinsterish editing... He gave himself so much unnecessary trouble altering 'breast' to 'shoulder,' 'flowers' to 'posies' or 'blossoms,' 'runnels' to 'rills,' 'pad' to 'path,' and 'naked lad' to 'merry bath.'" (In 1835, Taylor in proofreading *The Rural Muse,* wrote Clare that he must correct his theology by altering the phrase, "Death's long happy sleep" to "Heaven's eternal Peace," believing it better to have "Bad Divinity than good Atheism."[14])

By the fall of 1823 Clare was terribly depressed, and not only by the

---

[12]Naomi Lewis: *A Visit to Mrs. Wilcox* (Cresset Press, 1957)

[13]The full and accurate text, with notes, of *The Village Minstrel* may now be found in *The Early Poems of John Clare,* Vol. II, Eric Robinson and David Powell, eds. (Oxford, 1989)

[14]Quoted by Edward Storey, from Clare's correspondence

neglect of his publishers and the public. His was a mind that over-flowed "with excess of joys that spring from solitude," that treasured introspection and "speaking silence." He was confined to a tiny cottage swarming with little children and a ceaseless stream of words from a voluble wife. He was deeply in debt and suffering, like the children, from fen ague. Bloomfield had died, and so had his friend Gilchrist. Yet he kept writing exquisite poems, many of which would not be published for a hundred years, poems such as "The Nightmare" and "The Dream," which reveal his troubled mind. The latter poem contains a line worthy of Marvell or Browne: "When Time in terror drops his draining glass / And all things mortal, like to shadows, pass..." Poems of fragile beauty like "Evening Primrose": "Almost as pale as moonbeams are / or its companionable star..." And at the opposite extreme, romping ballads like "The Toper's Rant":

> Give me an old crone of a fellow
>   Who loves to drink ale in a horn
> And sing racy songs when hes mellow
>   which topers sang ere he was born
> For such a friend fate should be thanked
>   And line but our pockets with brass
> We'd sooner suck ale from a blanket
>   Than thimbles of wine thru a glass...

Then there is the final couplet of "Spring Morning," which sums up Clare as well as any lines he ever wrote:

> The flowers join lips below; the leaves above
> And every sound that meets the ear is love...

Clare's third book, *The Shepherd's Calendar,* came out in 1827. Robinson and Summerfield point out that Taylor, who had permitted many of Clare's dialect words to stand, "where they did not offend propriety" now "was slashing more vigorously, until almost all Clare's 'provincialisms' were replaced by words acceptable to London literary taste." Clare "strongly resented Taylor's treatment of the language... and it is ironic that two present-day editors of Clare (the Tibbles) should write approvingly of Taylor's truncated version: 'There are very few dialect words in *The Shepherd's Calendar,* and we find this deliberate part of his art almost perfected.'"[15]

But in 1964, Robinson and Summerfield's edition revealed the poem as it had never been seen before, and finally it had the chance of a fair appraisal. Elaine Feinstein praised the poem for its "remarkable intensity of physical sensation...What is celebrated throughout the poem is in some sense animal pleasure or release...full of an extraordinary exuberance which never fails to take into account the physical pressures of the life described."[16] Robinson and Summerfield say that the work is "a magnificent example of a sustained descriptive poem in the eighteenth century tradition. It is based on a month-by-month account of village and farming life, in which human and natural events are carefully interwoven..." It does not lend itself to brief excerpts.

Two years earlier, Clare noted in his diary a dream which proved prophetic:

> I had a very odd dream last night and I take it as an ill omen for I don't expect that the book will meet with a better fate. I thought I had one of the proofs of the new poems from London, and after looking at it awhile it shrank through my hands like sand, crumbling into dust...[17]

And indeed the book was a failure, selling but 400 copies in two years. Taylor made what proved to be a devastating suggestion: Clare should take over the remaining copies and sell them from door to door in the environs of Helpston. Clare was snubbed at every turn, particularly by those eager to humiliate one who had "got above his station."

Frantic for money, he turned to writing sentimental or patriotic verses for popular Annuals of the day with titles like *Friendship's Offering, Forget Me Not* and *The Amulet.* But more often than not these journals neglected to pay him. Clare was now deeply in debt; half-starved, his health continued to deteriorate, and most of his former

[15]From the introduction to *Selected Poems and Prose* (Oxford, 1966)
[16]Elaine Feinstein, ed. *John Clare: Selected Poems* (University Tutorial Press, 1868)
[17]Eric Robinson, ed. *John Clare's Autobiographical Writings* (Oxford, 1983)

fashionable and literary acquaintances had dropped away. Farmers in his own neighborhood refused to hire him as a laborer. He had, since childhood, been regarded as an eccentric, muttering to himself as he wandered, perhaps a poacher, perhaps, indeed, mad. He drank too much, he hung out with gypsies and other coarse companions, and he was too fond of the women. Then with his first success a good deal of malice and jealousy was aroused among his neighbors. Helpston had not forgiven him. "I live here among the ignorant like a lost man."[18]

At this dark hour Clare and his family were offered a cottage by the Fitzwilliams, three miles from Helpston at Northborough. Some of his finest poetry resulted from what was for him a traumatic change of environment. Many scholars have found his extreme sense of dislocation puzzling if not ludicrous. Although the new place was considerably larger, suited to the needs of his growing family, "there is a significant difference of atmosphere between the two places. One can see that the Northborough cottage did not have the same sense of belonging to its village as did the old place next to the Blue Bell Tavern . . . In the event the experience led to a series of carefully etched vignettes of rural life and rural isolation in which the poet constantly appears as the onlooker, the stranger, the outsider . . . snapshots of a way of life. The tension in these verses is so severe that the string of Clare's life seems about to break . . . "[19]

> Love's sun went down without a frown
> For very joy it used to grieve us
> I often think that west is gone
> Ah cruel time to undeceive us
> The stream it is a naked stream
> Where we on sundays used to ramble
> The sky hangs oer a broken dream
> The brambles nothing but a bramble
> O poesy is on the wane
> I cannot find her haunts again . . .

[18]*Letters*
[19]Eric Robinson and David Powell, *John Clare* (Oxford Authors Series, Oxford University Press, 1984)

In this excerpt from the poem, "Decay" in the line, "I often think that west is gone" one sees that Clare has even misplaced his sense of direction. Yes, the string of his life is growing very frayed indeed.

Yet the poems kept coming. Clare found the coins to buy a new notebook for a collection he wanted to call *A Midsummer Cushion,* after the name of a piece of turf covered with wildflowers with which the peasants decorated their cottages. One of his kindly, intrusive, proper-minded patronesses, a Mrs. Emmerson, insisted that the collection be called by the pedestrian title of *The Rural Muse.* It was published in 1835, sold poorly, and attracted very little attention. With its charming title restored, and one-third of the poems added which had been omitted from the 1835 edition, the book was republished 150 years later, edited by Mrs. Tibble and R.K.R. Thornton. Perhaps owing to the influence of her new collaborator – or the absence of her old one – Mrs. Tibble had mended her ways. The text was prepared from Clare's manuscript in the Peterborough Museum, "and is, as far as possible, an exact transcription of his own punctuation and spelling." However, maddeningly enough, the editors fail to indicate the poems which were omitted from the original publication.

Clare's life was falling apart. His mother died in 1835 and his father was living with the Clares and their seven children. Clare was showing more and more signs of mental instability, including his obsession with Mary Joyce who, he had come to believe, was his first wife and Patty his second. This cannot have contributed to harmony around the hearthside. (Mary Joyce, unmarried, was living but three miles away, but there is no indication that she and Clare had had any contact for many years.)

In 1837 he was committed to High Beach Asylum, in the charge of Dr. Matthew Allen, an unusually sympathetic and progressive physician. Clare was forty-four. In 1840, Dr. Allen wrote: "He has never been able to maintain in conversation, not even in writing prose, the appearance of sanity for two minutes or two lines together, and yet there is no indication whatever of insanity in any of his poetry." A visitor to High Beach in 1841, Cyrus Redding, has left us a sensitive description of Clare which was applicable to his mental state for the rest of his life: "The principal token of his mental eccentricity was the intro-

duction of prizefighting, in which he seemed to imagine he was to engage; but the allusion to it was made in the way of interpolation in the
middle of the subject on which he was discoursing, brought in
abruptly, and abandoned with equal suddenness . . . as if the machinery
of thought was dislocated, so that one part of it got off its pivot, and
protruded into the regular workings; or *as if a note had got into a piece of
music which had no business there.*" (My italics.)[20]

Though well-treated, Clare felt caged, and managed to run away in
1841. He has left us an extraordinary account of this three-day journey
during which he had nothing to eat but a handful of grass and a half-
pint of beer given him by a stranger on horseback. By the end of this
painful odyssey called "Journey out of Essex," Clare says that he was
met by a cart with a man and a woman and a boy in it: "the woman
jumped out and caught fast hold of my hands and wished me to get
into the cart but I refused and thought her either drunk or mad but
when I was told it was my second wife Patty I got in and was soon at
Northborough but Mary was not there . . ."[21]

Patty had hoped to keep him at home as he was no danger to anyone, but this proved impossible. He returned to High Beach for only a
few months. Dr. Allen believed that, given proper care, Clare could
have recovered, but a local doctor thought he knew better. One Dr.
Skrimshaw condemned him to the madhouse with the now infamous
phrase, "After years addicted to poetical prosings." This, fortunately
for posterity, was an addiction that nothing could cure. Clare was committed to the Northampton County Asylum, where he remained until
he died at age seventy.

Though Clare might have lived more contentedly at home, given
enough to eat and the assurance of minimum economic security, it is
difficult to believe that his slippery hold on his identity could have been
annealed. The poems tell us this more powerfully than the numerous
descriptions of Clare's conviction at various times that he was Shakespeare, Lord Byron or a noted prizefighter of the day:

---

[20]From *English Journal*, 1841, noted by Mark Storey in *Clare: The Critical Heritage*
(Routledge & Kegan Paul, 1973)
[21]Eric Robinson, ed. *John Clare's Autobiographical Writings* (Oxford University Press,
1983)

Say maiden wilt thou go with me
Through this sad non-identity
Where parents live and are forgot
And sisters live and know us not . . .

At once to be and not to be
That was, and is not—yet to see
Things pass like shadows—and the sky
Above, below, around us lie . . .

(from "An Invite to Eternity")

Or these lines from "I Am":

I am—yet what I am, none cares or knows;
   My friends forsake me like a memory lost:
I am the self-consumer of my woes;
   They rise and vanish in oblivion's host
Like shadows in love's frenzied stifled throes:
   And yet I am, and live—like vapours toss't
Into the nothingness of scorn and noise . . .

And from the magnificence of this to the pathos of this fragment:

Is nothing less than nought?
Nothing is is nought.
And there is nothing less.
But something is, though next to nothing
That a trifle seems: and such am I . . .

There are critics—notably Geoffrey Grigson, who edited *Poems of John Clare's Madness* in 1949—who believe that poetry from this period constitutes Clare's greatest work. But despite poems of undoubted genius such as "I Am" and "A Vision," most of the poems written during his incarceration lack some of the freshness, the immediacy of his vision, the glorious specifics of his earlier work. Yet there are flawless moments:

Are flowers the winter's choice
Is love's bed always snow . . .

I would trade the bulk of late nineteenth century poetry for that one couplet from "First Love." It has that quality unique to Clare which he describes in the first line of another very late poem, "I speak in low calm breathing whispers..."

Clare was well treated in the house of his second sequestration. He was given a good deal of freedom, especially in the earlier years, when he was allowed to wander in the village smoking his pipe and admiring pretty girls to whom he might write and dedicate a poem on the spot. He was always a little in love with all pretty women, and though Mary Joyce was first in time and first in intensity, "other Marys excited my admiration, & the first creator of my warm passions was lost in a perplexed multitude of names..."[22] The pages of his poems are strewn with the names of girls, girls, girls. My favorite: between two lines of a poem Clare has written the name of Ruth Popple Pilsgate.

Perhaps the only real luck of Clare's life was the kind treatment accorded him in both asylums, in a time when it was more usual to subject inmates to barbarous methods. The building where Clare stayed at the Northampton Asylum is still in use, like the Blue Bell Tavern, and is part of a private mental hospital, a handsome building in beautiful surroundings. The real hero of these years was the house steward of the asylum, W. F. Knight, who admired Clare's poetry, copied it out, and saved it. Two large volumes of Knight's transcriptions are in the Northampton Public Library.

Many, many of these poems are to Mary Joyce, whose death some years back Clare refused to accept.

> I sleep with thee and wake with thee
> And yet thou art not there:
> I fill my arms with thoughts of thee,
> And press the common air...

Mary, at first a human girl, then a Muse, then something like a Saint, is at last a Goddess, and the presiding deity of his life. Since 1984, Eric Robinson and David Powell have, with infinite and painstaking labor,

[22]*Autobiographical Writings*

transcribed from the original manuscripts the poems of Clare's love and madness. All the Marys, in mystery and metamorphosis, live in these two volumes of over a thousand pages.[23]

Still, though strong and healthy, given plenty to eat and excellent care, Clare was a prisoner, more closely held as the years went on, under a stricter management. And he knew where he was, in "the land of Sodom where all the people's brains are turned the wrong way." And he was unbearably lonely. One would like to believe that somewhere his soul may know of the devoted friends he is making these days, two hundred years after his birth.

[23]*The Later Poems of John Clare,* 2 vols. (Clarendon Press, 1984)

A Note on Robinson Jeffers

My PARENTS NEARLY NAMED ME Tamar. And it wasn't for the Biblical Tamar either, but for Robinson Jeffers's "heroine."

How could they consider naming a baby after a character who celebrated incest, perversity, arson, hysteria, deceit and what seems – Jeffers is rather opaque here – attempted murder? My decent parents celebrated none of the above – though who knows what violence lurks in the hearts of men and women to be catharsed by a dark genius such as Jeffers? But the impulse to name me Tamar (they must have decided that Tamar Kizer, with its motor-revving *r*s, was uneuphonious) sprang, I am quite sure, from their love of language:

> ...grave Orion
> Moved northwest from the naked shore, the moon moved to
> meridian, the slow pulse of the ocean
> Beat, the slow tide came in across the slippery stones...

That stately parade of *a* and *i* and *o* sounds, the luminous alliteration of those *m*s, the whole *andante* becoming slower and slower with the slow pulse and the slow tide, the meditative monosyllables, the alliterative sibilance of the ocean's motion...this is what would have named me.

I've often remarked, casually, that my mother read aloud to me from Whitman, Jeffers and Arthur Waley. She certainly read both "Tamar" and "Roan Stallion." Going back to these works after all these years, I am wonder-struck as to why she did it. These extremely violent poems – but more violent than the brothers Grimm or *Strewelpeter*? – were they dished out to me entire, or did Mother edit as she went along? Of course a great deal must have passed right over my head at the age of seven or eight or nine, particularly the passages dealing with incest and impregnation – and there are opacities in the writing here as well. But still . . . Coming back to Jeffers after a long absence is like being kicked in the gut. I suspect that with Mother and me there was a form of joint hypnosis: She had one of the world's most beautiful voices, and she must have cast a spell on us both, a spell of sounds in which meaning hovered somewhere in the middle distance, defused by music.

I look at Mother and Father's copy of *Dear Judas,* which they acquired in 1931, and read the marked passages, these from "The Loving Shepherdess": "Life glides by and the bright loving creatures/Eat us in the evening . . ." " . . . I wish that a Power went through the world/ And killed people at thirty when the ashes crust them," both spoken by the misanthropic old man to Vasquez: the mix of beautiful language and terrible message so characteristic of Jeffers, even when casting his misanthropy in the voice of one of his characters.

My parents have marked part of this passage from "The Broken Balance," and I would mark the rest:

> That light blood-loving weasel, a tongue of yellow
> Fire licking the sides of the gray stones,
> Has a more passionate and more pure heart
> In the snake-slender flanks than man can imagine;
> But he is betrayed by his own courage,
> The man who killed him is like a cloud hiding a star.
>
> Then praise the jewel-eyed hawk and the tall blue heron;
> The black cormorants that fatten their sea-rock
> With shining slime; even that ruiner of anthills
> The red-shafted woodpecker flying,
> A white star between blood-color wing-clouds,
> Across the glades of the wood and the green lakes of shade
>
> They live their felt natures; they know their norm
> and live it to the brim; they understand life . . .

It's that last couplet which my parents have marked, with a note by my father to say that this description of animal nature reminds him of D.H. Lawrence. Then in the poem Jeffers goes on to compare animals to men, to men's disadvantage, needless to say. As a poet, it is the descriptions of the birds and animals which I love in this passage, up to the sentimentality of Jeffers' claim that animals and birds understand life. It's clear to me that Theodore Roethke also loved this side of Jeffers: one hears cadences that must have haunted him: "the light blood-loving weasel" "licking the sides of the gray stones" and the brilliant compounds and spondees. (Anyone who doubts that Roethke read Jeffers with care – he is known to have taught him at Bennington – need only consult a speech near the end of "Dear Judas": "Money, money, money.")

"The Broken Balance" ends with another exquisite passage in a different cadence, which some call Whitmanesque:

> Under my windows, between the road and the sea-cliff, bitter
>   wild grass
> Stands narrowed between the people and the storm.
> The ocean winter after winter gnaws at its earth, the wheels
>   and the feet
> Summer after summer encroach and destroy.
> Stubborn green life, for the cliff-eater I cannot comfort you,
>   ignorant which color,
> Gray-blue or pale-green, will please the late stars . . .

Why do I remember this passage? The wild grass and the late stars, I suppose. The first poems I ever wrote, on the cusp of my teens, were full of spondees. Was this instinctive, or did I soak up such spondees from Jeffers? There are two more lines to the poem which rather spoil it for me, in the way that some of the most glorious psalms move from high lyricism to low revenge:

> But laugh at the other, your seed shall enjoy wonderful
>   vengeances and suck
> The arteries and walk in triumph on the faces.

Biblical indeed. But one may pay a price for picking up those psalmic cadences, though in my own case I hope not.

Perhaps everyone who knows Jeffers remembers best, "Shine, Perishing Republic." I've always held as an article of faith that it was a great poem, perhaps Jeffers' greatest. Again, I wonder what I made of it as a child. It is tempting to believe that I thought it was in the same mold as "The Battle Hymn of the Republic"! I suspect another kind of hypnosis from those rolling orotund phrases: It is intrinsic to the genius of the poem that Jeffers imitates the sounds of patriotism, the noise of national anthems, while the message of the poem is to shun political corruption: Take to the hills! Keep your distance from the human race:

> And boys, be in nothing so moderate as in love of man, a
> clever servant, insufferable master.
> There is the trap that catches noblest spirits, that caught —
> they say — God, when he walked on earth.

The ending is rather curious when one remembers that in "Dear Judas" the whole point of the poem/play comes from the mouth of Lazarus, speaking to Mary:

> Your son has done what men are not able to do;
> He has chosen and made his own fate . . .

Indeed, Christ chose to love without moderation, and made it his fate. It is hard not to wish that Jeffers had not hated mankind so fiercely, to the point where it deforms parts of his most distinguished work. But we have the rest, the dozens of beautiful shorter poems; we have the jewel-eyed hawk, the heron, the slow pulse of the ocean, the wild grass. And I have those memories of childhood, of being read to, in which Jeffers plays such a part — both the Jeffers that my mother and I imagined, and the true Jeffers who, like all great poets, grows along with us until maturity, when we meet face to face.

Western Space

WHENEVER THE SUBJECT of regional literature arises – particularly when the discussion concerns Western poetry – somehow the topic gets bogged down in botany: Desert versus slum; tree versus highrise, lilac versus transit system. Would Theodore Roethke have written so often about ferns if he had stayed in Pennsylvania? From there it's a short step to counting cactus in Richard Shelton, pines in Gary Snyder, salmon in William Stafford, steelhead in Richard Hugo. I see I have wandered from wildlife to fish, but the principle is the same. Although we Westerners tend to believe that we have a corner on wonderful place names – "Kittitas, Klickatat, TumTum and Pysht/This is the moment for which we have wished" (that is the voice of the late and too-neglected writer of light verse from Spokane: Stoddard King) – it wasn't one of us who wrote, "I have fallen in love with American names."

Although I have a rather different point to make here, I think it clarifies some of these problems to quote from the introduction, by Robin Skelton, to *Five Poets of the Pacific Northwest* (University of Washington Press, 1964). (The five were Kenneth Hanson, Richard Hugo, William Stafford, David Wagoner and myself.) It is a real tribute to Skelton – for many years now a resident of British Columbia, that this introduction holds up so well nearly three decades later. His selection of our poems was also extremely canny: he managed to pick out from the work of relatively young poets precisely those elements which were to emerge as major themes later on, and, in a way, to review what we were to become rather than what we were at the time – an act of real perception and generosity. Skelton said:

The poetry written in deserts and in cities, though it may refer to specific places, and even depend upon sympathy with some particular spot, rarely makes full use of natural imagery. That is to say, the perpetual interpenetration of the savage and the domestic, and the continual awareness of solitude, mortality and history do not present themselves inevitably in terms of landscape.

Solitude, mortality and history...It isn't entirely clear whether Skelton feels that these concerns are the property of all poets, or of Western poets most particularly.

Solitude: Yes. In big cities one is lonely. In the desert, the woods, in the small American town, the poet is solitary – and most of the time glad of it. Enormous spaces separate one poet from another. We write letters, mail poems; we befriend one another as best we can. Eastern visitors remark about our loyalties to one another, the pleasure we take in one another's success, the way we share unfinished work and ask for advice. "It isn't like that in New York!" they say. And the introspection encouraged by solitude is often more lyrical than sour, more sturdy than self-pitying.

Mortality: Once when Richard Hugo was asked what differentiated poets from other people, Dick replied, "Poets think about death *all the time.*" And I incline to the belief that Western writers have more intimations of mortality than Easterners, with the exception of those who live in big city areas where more and more often these days, children kill each other with guns. Most of us have seen the death of animals. (I am not counting road kill, about which Maxine Kumin has written so brilliantly.) Many of us have helped kill animals and birds, in the farmyard, or with a rifle in the woods. We are more apt to live with elderly people whom we have seen fail and die. And there is something about our great spaces – of desert and plains and fields, and the vast skies overhead – that makes us feel small, and fragile, and mortal. Whether we are more obsessed with solitude and death than poets living in the great spaces of T'ang Dynasty China (greater than now because of the enormous difficulties of travel) or the Russian poets of the first half of this century is arguable. It seems to me that Mandelstam, Akhmatova, Tsvetayeva – though they suffered, understandably, from a *moral* claustrophobia, have a spaciousness lacking in the poets of Eastern Europe who, though perhaps equally gifted in some cases, seem constricted by the size of their countries.

So far as history is concerned – Skelton's third point – I am less sure. I don't believe that writers in other parts of the country can compete with the Southerners when it comes to obsession with history. Let me make one big exception here: American Indian writers, Japanese and Chinese Americans, and Chicana and Chicano writers. The parallels are obvious: Killing and loss – not only the loss of a war or wars, but the loss of a way of life: these are matters not easily or perfunctorily dealt with, or dismissed in one generation or two, because the toll goes on. There are dangers in so much retrospection, dangers to the writer him/ herself, but on balance I think our literature has been immeasurably enriched – *fertilized* – by flesh and bone and blood, and there is a *mort* of unfinished business: they have just begun to fight. (As for Black writers, the situation is quite different: They desperately search for lost history, and when fragments fail, they are forced to invent.)

For us of the West, history for the most part is what happened yesterday. We share with native Americans the words of Chief Joseph of the Nez Perce: "Our chiefs are tired of fighting. Looking Glass is dead. The old men are killed. It is the young men who say yes or no. He who led the young men is dead. It is cold and we have no blankets. Our little children are freezing to death. I want time to look for my children and see how many of them I may find . . . Hear me, my chiefs, I am tired. Heart is sick and sad. From where the sun now stands, I will fight no more forever."

And our other great poet, Chief Seattle (Sealth), with a dignity as marmoreal as that of the great Roman writers: "When the last Red Man shall have perished, and the memory of my tribe shall have become a myth among the white man, these shores will swarm with the invisible dead of my tribe; and when your children's children think themselves alone in the field, the store, the shop, upon the highway, or in the silence of the pathless woods, they will not be alone . . . At night when the streets of your cities are silent and you think them deserted, they will throng with the returning hosts that once filled them and still love this beautiful land . . . " Solitude, mortality and history. And the blood guilt that we of the West must carry, all our days.

We are marked by the events of forty-nine – 1849 – the search for gold, the ramshackle towns, some of them sprung to life virtually overnight, to be the purveyors of food and drink – and sex – for the miners, loggers, trappers; camp cooks for the railroad builders, itinerant laborers, farmers and traders; the fly-by-night entrepreneurs that follow on the heels of those who have set out to tame a new country. Tame, rape, exploit, develop, civilize, destroy: pick your words.

Where I come from was once characterized by the phrase, "the forty-seven states and the Soviet of Washington." For along with the land-fighters, claim-stakers and post-diggers came the owners and bosses-to-be; the struggles of union organizers, fire-breathing radicals – some of them women – with their smudgy pamphlets and bulky handpresses; laborer-poets like Charles Ashley, and the half-educated, self-educated men and women who pored over Shakespeare and Shelley by the light of an oil lamp. And then came the strikebreakers, the Pinkerton men, the hired posses and private armies of the mine-owners, lumber barons and railroad kings.

More than eighty years ago, my mother was an organizer for the I.W.W. During the terrible Pinkerton riots in Seattle, she was working for Anna Louise Strong who edited *The Union Record*. The building that housed the paper was set on fire (arson by guess who?) and Mother loved to tell of how she lost her presence of mind and ran down eight flights of stairs lugging Ms. Strong's ancient typewriter, which must have weighed forty pounds or more, while the important papers in the office were consumed in the conflagration. A decade later she was working for the government (how times have changed! Imagine an ex-radical working for the *government* any time during the last fifty years) investigating the conditions of women and children in the mining and lumber camps of the Northwest, when she met my father in Spokane and married him. I grew up on her stories of these times and was nourished by her glorious, never-fading indignation.

This, or variations of it, is the past with which we live, the space which we inhabit. But I don't mean to suggest that we write about it. For the most part we don't, although writers like John Keeble and William Kittridge do magnificent work in this territory. But we are haunted by this past of ours – and I include those who have migrated to the West and who have lived here so long that they are more western than we natives. We all live with the vision of an Eden despoiled. In a very literal sense we live with images of rack and ruin. To inhabit what was once a magnificent wilderness, with its extraordinary variety of landscape: the magic silences of the rain forest, the desert with its thousands of varieties of wildflowers carpeting the earth in early spring ("belly-flowers" they're called), the great rolling wheat-fields, lion-tawny in summer, and in winter the chocolate colored soil striped with snow, after ploughing: the thousands of lakes, the river which my father always saluted with the identical words, "Here's the mighty Columbia – it's a noble stream"; the Snake River, so perfectly named in its sinuous twistings, still so little known; the mountains: that mountain, perfect as Fujiyama, which we will never see again; the fabulous coast, great boulders which sit in foaming water; the cypress twisted by wind, the madrona with trunks like the skin of Gauguin's women – to suffer the incursions and depredations of indifferent men, or giant corporations run by people who may never have seen the land and water they so casually spoil. To live in the midst of this is to live, in some sense, like a fallen angel who sees paradise taken from him piece by piece, not by God but by man. This must account in part for the wry detachment of William Stafford, a smoky air of sweetness and loss. It accounts, in part, for David Wagoner's grasping at Indian legend and myth, part reconstruction, part invention: the impulse to conserve, to memorialize what is lost, to elegize what is dying before our eyes. In my own case, I think it is responsible for a kind of savagery, self-directed more often than not, a highly developed sense of irony mixed with an impulse to elegize – because a way to deal with loss is to raise the shield of bitter laughter – all this in the midst of a quality we all share: an exuberance, despite everything, because this is the great big West, where we can still fling out our arms, sing and shout without being arrested – except perhaps in Los Angeles. In the midst of mourning, we still have lots of space in which to move around, alone in the field, with our ghosts.

Poetic Space:
Richard Shelton

WITH THE PUBLICATION OF *Selected Poems* (University of Pittsburgh Press, 1982) Richard Shelton should be acknowledged as in the first rank of American poets. However, for a long time now there have been a number of his poems preserved and cherished by his peers: poems such as the moving and passionate, "Requiem for Sonora"; "Dream of Return," the best poem about homecoming since Frost said they had to let you in; and the hallucinated brilliance – Kafka in a five-gallon hat – of his prose poem, "The Bus to Veracruz." But Shelton's appeal extends to those for whom poetry is an alien form, not a habit. Like Galway Kinnell, and Whitman before them, he is a poet who can appeal to virtually anyone, if he's given a chance. He writes of concerns we have in common with power and clarity, although there is no doubt that his habitat is Arizona, and that he is in love with it.

When he began writing, Shelton was bemused by French Surrealism, and some of his poetry from that period has a contrived and bookish air. (That Shelton is aware of this seems indicated by his severe culling of early work for his *Selected Poems*.) However, one can be grateful for his schooling in Surrealism because, over the years, he has applied it to what might be called the surrealism of everyday life. What Gaston Bachelard has named, "a drama of images" is transformed into a perverse or black comedy of images, appropriate to describing life as we know it in the last gasp of the twentieth century. For example, take this poem, "History":

always on the horizon someone
is holding up a red thing
like a butchered cow its eyes
are as distant as old photographs

we invent the past we give it
to anyone who happens along it is
a bottomless lake with only
one shore and near it
we build our contradictions
towers with both clocks and bells
steps leading up to a blind wall

I do not understand war or history

the signs read *this way out*
it is a long way and there were
so many people I loved so many
people I could have loved

There is a straight looking, an unflinchingness in this, as in much of his work – a quality rather rare in American poetry, although we find it in abundance in the writing of Eastern European poets such as Herbert and Popa. Shelton resembles them in other ways as well: the method of setting up a poem, the minimalism, the syntactical shortcuts. Like them, Shelton has a highly developed tragic sense which seems, by evidence in his work, to have evolved from a wretched childhood.

But the quality which sets Shelton apart from his peers, is his relation to space. Perhaps that is what distinguishes the Western writer most of all. Shelton may be used as a living illustration of many of the points which Bachelard makes in *The Poetics of Space,* that philosophic handbook for artists and architects of my generation. In the introduction to that great work, Bachelard speaks of the "simple images of felicitous space," and that he seeks "to determine the human value of the sorts of space that may be grasped, that may be defended against adverse forces, the space we love." In "Sonora for Sale," Shelton writes:

we come down a white road in the moonlight
dragging our feet like innocents

to find the guilty already arrived
and in possession of everything...

we are here we cannot turn back
soon we hold out our hands
full of money
this is the desert
it is all we have left to destroy

And again, in his great elegy for the desert, "Requiem for Sonora":

years ago I came to you as a stranger
and have never been worthy
to be called your lover or to speak your name
loveliest
most silent sanctuary
more fragile than forests
more beautiful than water...

I have learned to accept
whatever men choose to give me
or whatever they choose to withhold
but oh my desert
yours is the only death I cannot bear

Bachelard says that daydreaming, when it contemplates grandeur, creates an attitude so special, an inner state so unlike any other, that the daydream transports the dreamer "to a world that bears the mark of infinity." In Shelton's case, this state is more often night-dreaming, alone in the Sonora desert, in the awareness of this "intimate immensity." At these times, "he is no longer shut up in his own weight, the prisoner of his own being." This condition is desperately important to Shelton the poet, who so often feels imprisoned by his body, his face, and what he sees as his personal failures. In "Out Here," a recent poem,

when the moon rises
and Sonora is covered
with silence brilliant as snow
I walk into a dream unafraid...

out here nothing needs me
nothing fails me I lie down
in the bed of an arroyo
look at the stars and forget
. . . all the rest

when there is nothing left
I remember the precision
of the hummingbird piercing
the dark heart of the hibiscus
and doing no damage

I begin to hear night
breathing through me promising
that death does not last forever
and teaching me
the secret names of the stars

To quote Gaston Bachelard a final time: "When a poet knows that a living thing in the world" – and a desert is a living thing – "is in search of its soul, this means that he is in search of his own." There is more, much more, to be said of Richard Shelton's poetry than is possible in this brief review. But I hope I have indicated some of the qualities which make him of such value, ways in which, to paraphrase Rilke, Shelton's outer space and inner space meet, and encourage each other to go on growing.

The Poetics of Water:
A Sermon

AT THE BEGINNING OF the beginning, that is, at Genesis, we know by heart that the Spirit of God moved upon the face of the Waters. Before light, before the sun of consciousness, there was darkness upon the face of the deep. We are in the formless void, in the primordial time before definition, division, discrimination.

Water is the time-honored, time-antiquated symbol of the instinctual, the intuitive, the unconscious, inevitably linked to the feminine principle, tied to the moon and to all the fructifying powers of life. In Hildegarde of Bingen's *Hymn to the Holy Ghost* which begins: "O Ignius, Spiritus, Paraclete" we read, "From you the clouds rain down, the heavens move,/the stones have their moisture, the waters give forth streams/and the earth sweats out greenness." (A wonderful phrase worthy of Donne!)

It has been said that the Holy Spirit as we conceive it is a product of Latin grammar – Spiritus is masculine – and, as Robert Graves has put it, "is born of the early Christian mistrust of the female principle."

The ascetic Essenes-Ebionites believed in a female Holy Spirit. Certainly in its power of healing, life-giving and nourishing, the Spirit can readily be intuited as feminine. This interpretation of the Holy Spirit as feminine needs to be revalidated and reinvigorated in our time to bring into balance the moral and social forces that are so heavily weighted on the side of a thousand years of overweening masculine power. These are not abstractions that we are talking about today. We are talking about the forces of materialism and the rational which have brought us into such a perilous state, which have damaged life sources, the land

and food which is needed for our survival, forces which threaten us with extinction.

Water is traditionally known to be the source of generation. In primitive belief Water could fertilize a virgin who could bring forth young. These were the daughters and sons of river deities, of the seas and of the great ocean itself. Many are the myths in which the divine child is found upon the river bank. One of the peculiar aspects of this prime element whose symbol is the sea is that symbolically floating on it or rising out of it means the same thing. Both imply a state of being not yet separated from non-being *yet still being.* These divinities are "in the womb of the universe floating in their embryonic state on the primal waters."

Most of us are familiar with the Egyptian and Greek myths and in some degree with those of the Indian and Chinese traditions which help to validate these archetypal foundations of our own faith. It is known that the Lao-tzu text abounds in female imagery. The Tao itself is no abstract entity but rather a great mother, the waters of an eternal womb from which emerge all the particular entities that populate the ephemeral world. The text says, "It is the mother of all under Heaven. I do not know its name but I style it way-shower or Tao." The imagery which attempts to flesh out this entity is aqueous and implies a female, all-enveloping ocean of fertility, something like the Babylonian goddess Tiamat. Analogies are readily made with Ishtar, a mother goddess and daughter of the ocean stream, and with Isis, a fertility and river goddess, ruler of the Nile's flood; with Aphrodite and with St. Mary of Egypt whose origin, like that of all the Marys, is pelagic or pertaining to the ocean or distant seas. The Virgin Mary herself was, to the Gnostics, Mare (of the sea). "Ave Maris stella" are the opening words of an ancient hymn to Mary.

Ishtar of Babylon, the moon goddess, was giver of rain, not only the gentle rain of spring which made the crops grow but sometimes of the devastating downpours of August which destroyed the crops. Particular rites were established to pray to the goddess to withhold those harvest storms. This came to correspond with the feast of the Assumption of the Blessed Virgin, who is particularly asked to turn aside storms until the fields had been reaped. A passage from a Syriac text of *The De-*

parture of My Lady from this World runs, "And the apostles ordered that there should be a commemoration of the blessed one on the thirteenth of Ab (August) on account of the trees bearing bunches of grapes and on account of the trees bearing fruit, that the clouds of hail, bearing stones of wrath, might not come, and the trees be broken and their fruits and the vines with their clusters."

Now Water is not only the water of origin, the water of life, but it is also the water of retribution as God warned Noah, and as Ishtar, the Moon Goddess, the mother of Ra, mourned and condemned and saved a remnant of her people with these words: "I, the mother, have begotten my people and like the young fishes they fill the sea; the gods concerning the spirits were weeping with me; six days and nights passed, the wind, the deluge, the storms overwhelmed. On the seventh day in its course was calmed the storm and all the deluge which had destroyed like an earthquake quieted." Like Noah, on the seventh day: "in the course of it I sent forth a dove and it left." In the Old Testament story Noah, informed by a dove which is a bird invariably associated with moon and water deities, came safety to land. There is a Chinese myth of the Great Flood in which the moon goddess sends her representative to earth, after the waters have subsided, to repeople the world.

Vast amounts of time and research have been expended in trying to connect an historical flood with the events of Noah. The Hindus, who were more psychologically oriented than the Hebrews or the Egyptians, recognized the flood story as representing stages of consciousness or psychological development. The ark, which in Hindi means crescent or moonboat, carries the soul to the new world, to a new life. It is the boat of immortality. As Bachelard puts it, "for some dreamers, water is the new movement that beckons toward a journey never made . . ." Such astonishing grandeur is contained in these lines of Baudelaire: "Oh death, ancient captain, the time has come!/Let us weigh anchor!"

The legend of the boat of the dead is one of the earliest to be noted in the folklore of France: In the middle of the night, fishermen's families hear a knocking at the door; they get up and find strange boats along the shore, so loaded down that they sink, their gunwales scarcely a thumb's width above the water. No matter in what legend we find the account, the boats loaded with dead are on the verge of sinking. It

is an astonishing image, in which Death is afraid of dying. The weight
of the boat is so heavy because the souls are weighted with sin.

Here we find a plangent echo in the poetry of D.H. Lawrence with
the accepting serenity of a man about to die:

And it is time to go, to bid farewell
to one's own self, and to find an exit
from the fallen self.

Have you built your ship of death, O have you?
O build your ship of death, for you will need it.

*   *   *

Build then the ship of death, for you must take
the longest journey, to oblivion.
And die the death, the long and painful death
that lies between the old self and the new.

Already the dark and endless ocean of the end
is washing in through the breaches of our wounds,
already the flood is upon us.

*   *   *

Now launch the small ship, now as the body dies
and life departs, launch out, the fragile soul
in the fragile ship of courage, the ark of faith
with its store of food and little cooking pans
and change of clothes,
upon the flood's black waste
upon the waters of the end
upon the sea of death, where still we sail
darkly, for we cannot steer, and have no port.

*   *   *

The flood subsides, and the body, like a worn sea shell
emerges strange and lovely.
And the little ship wings home, faltering and lapsing
on the pink flood,
and the frail soul steps out, into her house again
filling the heart with peace.

*   *   *

Jung has said:

> Whoever looks into the mirror of the water will see first of all his own face. Whoever goes into himself risks a confrontation with himself. It is the world of water where all life floats in suspension, where the realm of the sympathetic system, the soul of everything living, begins. Where I am indivisible this *and* that. Where I experience the other in myself, and the other than myself experiences me. Our concern with the unconscious has become a vital question for us — a question of spiritual being or non-being. All those who have had experience of it know that the treasure lies in the depths of the waters and will try to salvage it.

Now I should like to discuss a poem of my own, written some time ago, called "A Muse of Water":

> We who must act as handmaidens
> To our own goddess, turn too fast,
> Trip on our hems, to glimpse the muse
> Gliding below her lake or sea,
> Are left, long staring after her,
> Narcissists by necessity;
>
> Or water-carriers of our young
> Till waters burst, and white streams flow
> Artesian, from the lifted breast;
> Cup-bearers then, the tiny gods,
> Imperious table-pounders, who
> Are final arbiters of thirst.
>
> Fasten the blouse, and mount the steps
> From kitchen taps to Royal Barge,
> Assume the trident, don the crown,
> Command the Water Music now
> That men bestow on Virgin Queens;
>
> Or, goddessing above the waist,
> Appear as swan on Thames or Charles
> Where iridescent foam conceals
> The pedal-stroke beneath the glide;
> Immortal feathers preened in poems!

Not our true, intimate nature, stained
By labor, and the casual tide.

Masters of civilization, you
Who moved to river banks from cave,
Putting up tents, and deities,
Through every rivulet wander through
The final unpolluted glades
To cinder-bank and culvert-lip,

And all the pretty chatterers
Still round the pebbles as they pass
Lightly over their water course,
And even the calm rivers flow,
We have, while springs and skies renew,
Dry wells, dead seas, and lingering drouth.

Water itself is not enough.
Harness her turbulence to work
For man: fill his reflecting pools.
Drained for his cofferdams, or stored
In reservoirs for his personal use:
Turn switches! Let the fountains play!

And yet these buccaneers still kneel
Trembling at the water's verge;
"Cool River-Goddess, sweet ravine,
Spirit of pool and shade, inspire!"
So he needs poultice for his flesh.
So he needs water for his fire.

We rose in mists and died in clouds
Or sank below the trammeled soil
To silent conduits underground,
Joining the blind-fish, and the mole.
A gleam of silver in the shale:
Lost murmur! Subterranean moan!

So flows in dark caves, dries away,
What would have brimmed from bank to bank,

Kissing the fields you turned to stone,
Under the boughs your axes broke.
And you blame streams for thinning out,
Plundered by man's insatiate want?

Rejoice when a faint music rises
Out of a brackish clump of weeds,
Out of the marsh at ocean-side,
Out of the oil-stained river's gleam,
By the long causeways and grey piers
Your civilizing lusts have made.

Discover the deserted beach
Where ghosts of curlews safely wade:
Here the warm shallows lave your feet
Like tawny hair of magdalens
Here, if you care, and lie full length,
Is water deep enough to drown.

In this poem, as in many others, water is not only an instrument of reflection, it is a symbol of reflection.

"Where is reality?" Bachelard asks, "in the sky or in the depths of the water? Infinite in our dreams is as high in the firmament as it is deep beneath the waves." Such double images are like "the hinges of a dream . . . At this juncture, water grasps the sky. Through dreams, water comes to signify that most distant Home, the celestial one."

Water, by its reflection, doubles the world – it also doubles the dreamer. This is beautifully expressed by the seventeenth century metaphysical poet, Thomas Traherne, in these stanzas:

> . . . Thus did I by the Water's brink
> Another World beneath me think;
> And while the lofty spacious Skies
> Reversed there abus'd mine Eys,
>   I fancy'd other Feet
>   Came mine to touch or meet;
> As by som Puddle I did play
> Another World within it lay.

Beneath the Water People drown'd,
Yet with another Hev'n crown'd,
In spacious Regions seem'd to go
As freely moving to and fro:
    In bright and open Space
    I saw their very face;
Eys, Hands, and Feet they had like mine;
Another sun did with them shine.

'Twas strange that Peeple there should walk,
And yet I could not hear them talk:
That throu a little watry Chink,
Which one dry Ox or Horse might drink
    We other Worlds should see,
    Yet not admitted be;
And other Confines there behold
Of Light and Darkness, Heat and Cold . . .

By walking Men's reversed Feet
I chanc'd another World to meet;
Tho it did not to View exceed
A Phantasm, 'tis a World indeed,
    Where Skies beneath us shine,
    And Earth by Art divine
Another face presents below,
Where People's feet against Ours go . . .

O ye that stand upon the Brink,
Whom I so near me, throu the Chink,
With Wonder see: What faces there,
Whose Feet, whose Bodies, do ye wear?
    I my Companions see
    In You, another Me.
They seemed Others, but are We;
Our second Selvs those Shadows be . . .

Of all the Play-mates which I knew
That here I do the Image view
In other Selvs; what can it mean?
But that below the purling Stream
    Som unknown Joys there be

Laid up in Store for me;
To which I shall, when that thin Skin
Is broken, be admitted in . . .

The functional aspect of the supercelestial waters of Genesis is a sort of baptismal water which possesses a creative and transforming quality. Aquinas said, "Water is the living grace of the holy spirit." Bruno, Bishop of Wurzburg, said, "Flowing water is the holy spirit." Garnerius of St. Victor, "Water is the infusion of the holy spirit." Divine water is said to effect a transformation by bringing the hidden nature to the surface. And in the Treatise of Comarius we find the miraculous waters that produce a new springtime.

The Church still performs the rite of the Benedictia Fontes on Holy Saturday before Easter. The rite consists of the repetition of the *De sensus spiritus sancti in aqua*. Ordinary water thereby acquires the divine quality of transforming and giving spiritual rebirth to man.

In Revelations XII we read:

And he showed me a pure river of water of life, clear as crystal, proceeding out of the throne of God and of the Lamb. In the midst of the street of it, and on either side of the river, was there the tree of life, which bare twelve manner of fruits, and yielded her fruit every month and the leaves of the tree were for the healing of the nations. And there shall be no more curse.

Here the maternal significance of water is one of the clearest interpretations of symbols in the whole field of mythology. The sea is the symbol of generation. From water comes life. Hence Mithras is represented as having been born beside a river, as was Moses, while Christ experienced his rebirth in the Jordan River. All living things rise like the sun and sink into it again at evening. Born of springs, rivers, lakes and seas, man at death comes to the waters of the Styx and there embarks on the night-sea journey. These black Waters of death are the Waters of life, for death with its cold embrace is the maternal womb just as the seed is the Sun that brings it forth again. Life knows no death.

The projection of the image of the mother upon Water endows it with numinous and magical qualities associated with the mother. For example, the baptismal Water symbolism, Jonah and the Whale. Sea or a large body of water signifies the unconscious because it can be associated with the mother or matrix of consciousness.

Saint John says that Jesus answered Nicodemus thus: "Verily, verily I say unto thee, except a man be born of water and of the spirit he cannot enter into the kingdom of God." Now the manifest content of the reference to Water clearly has to do with baptism in the mind of John writing considerably after the event. But I believe that it is not only sound theology but sound intuition as well to interpret Jesus's remarks as linking together Water and Spirit.

As in Genesis, the Spirit is *upon* the Water and *of* the Water. Nicodemus asking, "How can a man be born when he is old? Can he enter a second time into his mother's womb?" is being literal-minded, didactic and fidgety. He is linear and trapped in time: If you are old how can you be born?

But Christ is calm. A calm of one who exists in the timeless, universal, the everlasting now, in the certainty of God's abiding love as long as we are serenely confident of our origins in the Watery embrace of the Father-Mother God.

So Big: An Essay on Size

I'M SOMETHING OVER 5'10" in my bare feet, and I look, as I've often remarked, like a road-company Valkyrie, but I have the soul of a brown sparrow. My friends guffaw. The general belief is that anyone over 5'6" can't possibly by shy. *Very thin* people who are tall may be able to get away with a certain amount of foot-scuffling and aw-shucksing, but anyone else in the large, economy package is out of luck.

I know an enormous architect who suffers, as I do, at big parties where we don't know many people. When I asked how he coped, he said, "I just sort of stand there and *loom*." This makes him resemble a national monument, and people come over to inspect him.

Getting slightly liquored up sometimes helps, and we've tried that. But most of the time I fall back on the bookshelves (not actually – I'm not *that* liquored up) and the chair in the corner with the reading lamp. If you're small, people come sit on the arm of your chair and draw you out. If you're me, they assume that you're some kind of a snob, or aloof, or just trying to attract attention.

Alternatively, I strike up conversations with bartenders. These experienced people can spot shyness better than most. And, when truly desperate, I've been known to collect ashtrays and used glasses, and help wash up. Does anyone sympathize? No.

My mother was trained in nutrition, among other things. And coming from a family that had been decimated by tuberculosis, she feared that I might contract it. So virtually from birth I was over-vitaminized. Consequently, I was a large child, and by the time I hit first grade I was easily a head taller than anyone else, and stayed that way for years. (We will draw the veil over my adolescence, painful enough if you're average.)

Later in life, I travelled in both China and Japan, where children used to follow me in the streets shouting remarks which I was undoubtedly fortunate not to understand. But that old feeling returned, which I remembered from first grade: I am an albino giraffe. Keep in mind the legendary shyness of that species and you'll come closer to understanding your outsize friends.

My mother understood, being herself tall (for her generation), shy, and additionally cursed with the name of Mabel. "Mabel," a kind hostess said to her, as she hovered near the doorway of a room where her young peers were chattering away, "why don't you go in and make conversation?"

"Can't think of anything to say," Mother mumbled.

"Tell a joke."

"Don't know any jokes."

"Well, ask them why Grover Cleveland wears red, white and blue suspenders."

"Why *does* Grover Cleveland wear red, white and blue suspenders?" Mother wanted to know.

"To hold his trousers up, silly. Now go *in* there," the nice hostess said, giving her a gentle shove. So Mother stalked into the room, which immediately fell silent, and blurted out, "Why does Grover Cleveland wear red, white and blue suspenders to hold his trousers up?"

It broke the ice all right, and sixty years later she laughed about it, but you could sense the trauma.

When I had daughters of my own, I tended to limit their intake of milk and orange juice, and the confetti of vitamin pills which littered the dining-room table of my childhood had no place on theirs. So they are as tall and beautiful as my mother was, but they are not on my level by any means.

Now the nutritional information once limited to rare specialists like my mother is widespread, and until recently fewer people have gone hungry in their growing years. When I ride in elevators these days I am often able to look the younger of my fellow-inmates in the eye. It's a comfort.

As a girl, I sympathized with Mrs. Roosevelt, and the valiant efforts she made to force herself out of herself—not only tall, but awkward, and, as she thought, plain. However, she acquired that lovely gift, as my shy mother did in maturity: concern for others swallows up concern for self, and shyness evaporates. That this concern eventually made Mrs. Roosevelt into a beauty must have been the furthest thing from her mind. But it gave a great deal of satisfaction to a great many people.

With these two examples before me, I think I have learned to be comfortable with all sorts of people, and to extend some comfort to those in need of it. The problem is parties, with people who look more secure than I feel. I'm the kind of person who goes to a party overflowing with the glamorous and interesting whom I would die to know, and who automatically heads for the limp little man standing by the fireplace twisting his wineglass and wishing he were dead. Every party has a loser, and I always find him. (All right, or *her.*)

After the first hour or so—which is usually about fifteen minutes—I am cursing myself as I say, "Yes, do go on," in soothing tones, and look wildly for the bartender. This perhaps is a reason why I get chummy with the purveyors of vinous spirits.

"Did you ever meet T.S. Eliot?" people ask me. "Did you ever meet Sylvia Plath?" Well, yes, I was introduced. But I wasn't having a conversation with either. I passed the hour with someone who had prenasal drip and had just lost his job on a magazine. Or I was spending an inordinate amount of time in the ladies' room with a desperate fat girl whose dress had just split its seams.

Of course I don't always seek them out. I attract them too. If you look like a human wailing wall, what can you expect? If you are 5′2″, and you buy your dresses in the junior department, people don't think you are a) their mother, b) The White Goddess, or c) The Spirit of Christmas Past. Oh well. It has its moments. I've chatted up a couple of basketball teams on airplanes. I find it easy to talk to John Kenneth Galbraith (although to be fair, you don't have to be tall, just a woman). And, as with the Lincoln Memorial, little children like to climb onto my lap.

Gentlemen Songsters

JOHN BERRYMAN

ONE WONDERS WHY *Dream Song, the Life of John Berryman* (Morrow, 1990) was written. A biography of John Berryman by John Haffenden was published as recently as 1982 and covered the same territory. It was not quite as inclusive and intrusive regarding irrelevant personal details; mercifully, it was nearly seventy pages shorter and considerably better written than Paul Mariani's *Dream Song*. Both writers agree that the suicide of Berryman's father, John Allyn Smith, in 1926 when his son was not yet twelve years old, was the trauma that shadowed Berryman's life until he followed suit.

However, in 1970 Berryman surprised himself by noting: "Have I been wrong all these years, and it was *not* Daddy's death that blocked my development for so long? . . . So maybe my long self-pity has been based on an *error,* and there has been no (hero-) villain (Father) ruling my life, but only an unspeakably powerful possessive adoring MOTHER." Mr. Haffenden's account of the mother's influence is fuller than Mr. Mariani's; for example, he tells us that after John had been in prep school just over a month, she had written him twenty-seven letters. Vain, sexy—she liked to tell strangers that John and his brother Bob were her brothers—a nonstop talker, even in old age, according to Berryman, she still led a life wholly centered on him.

Still, it was the father's suicide that prompted some of Berryman's most powerful "Dream Songs" as well as prefiguring his own death. "Dream Song 235," in memory of Hemingway, ends:

> Save us from shotguns & fathers' suicides.
> It all depends on who you're the father of
> if you want to kill yourself—
> a bad example, murder of oneself,
> the final death, in a paroxysm of love
> for which good mercy hides? . . .
>
> Mercy! my father; do not pull the trigger
> or all my life I'll suffer from your anger
> killing what you began.

Or consider the second stanza of "Dream Song 384":

> I spit upon this dreadful banker's grave
> who shot his heart out in a Florida dawn
> O ho alas alas
> When will indifference come, I moan & rave
> I'd like to scribble till I got right down
> away down under the grass
>
> and ax the casket open ha to see
> just how he's taking it.

The poem ends with the terrible image of the poet tearing apart the mouldering grave clothes and taking the axe to the corpse.

Berryman's mother evidently had an affair with a neighbor, John Angus Berryman, before Smith's suicide. Then she married John Angus, who adopted John and his younger brother (the name change being another source of John's guilt). Both biographies are similar in their treatment of Berryman's life through school and college. It's pretty much the standard rite of passage for young males growing up in the 1930's—silliness, booze and girls, the distinctive feature being Berryman's outrage when close friends stole his women and the way in which he did the same thing to his friends without seeming to notice the parallel behavior.

When Berryman was twenty-one, Columbia University gave him a fellowship to study at Cambridge. One is tempted to think that his mastery of English syntax, unequalled in my opinion by any other American poet, was perfected in Britain when the English still knew how to educate people, but this topic remains for another commentator. While abroad, Berryman met Yeats, Auden (only seven years older and already internationally famous) and Eliot. But his strongest bond was with Dylan Thomas, who shared his own dangerous attraction to drink and debauchery. Berryman came home two years later on the Ile-de-France with an English umbrella in one hand and a book in the other and a bogus English accent that annoyed his friends.

But for fans of Berryman's poetry things get more interesting in the early forties when Berryman married his first wife, Eileen, became friends with Delmore Schwartz and Robert Lowell and was taken under the wing of Richard Blackmur at Princeton. In 1936 Blackmur had written something in *Poetry* magazine which Berryman was never to forget: the art of poetry is "amply distinguished from the manufacture of verse by the animating presence in the poetry of a fresh idiom: language so twisted and posed in a form that it not only expresses the matter at hand but adds to the stock of available reality."

Mr. Mariani's account of the Berrymans' ups and downs, emotional and financial, his job insecurities, his repeated attempts at literary projects, most of them aborted, are summed up in a letter to his mother on turning thirty: "My talent lost, like my hair" – he still had plenty of hair when he died, twenty-eight years later – "sex crumbling like my scalp. Disappointment & horror. . . . Everything begun . . . everything abandoned. Every day I wish to die." Considering his flagrant marital infidelities of this period, perhaps it is a pity that his sex had not crumbled even further.

But what matters to us is the poetry, and one of his affairs had inspired a series of sonnets that he dared not show Eileen (they were published in 1967 as "Berryman's Sonnets"):

> I see I do, it must, trembling I see
> Grace of her switching walk away from me
> Fastens me where I stop now, smiling pain;
> And neither pride don nor the fever shed
> More, till the furor when we slide to bed.

Lowell has left us a sunnier Berryman than the man reflected in his letter to his mother – all "ease and light" revealing his intense familiarity with all of Shakespeare and pointing out "what could be done with disrupted and mended syntax." In turn, Berryman defended Lowell from an imputation of plagiarism that appeared in the *New Yorker* in 1947: "The poet invents some of his materials, and others he takes where he finds them, – from personal, conversational and literary experience; what he gives them is air order, rhythm, significance, and he does this by means of style and the inscrutable operation of personality."

A few months later, in the *Partisan Review,* while denying Eliot's theory of the impersonality of the poet, Berryman wrote: "One observes a certain desire in the universities to disinfect Mr. Eliot by ignoring his disorderly and animating associations" (hardly a conventional assessment of Eliot at that time). He went on to say that Eliot's mind was "grievous and profound beyond a single poet's" and that in the end his poetry, "which the commentators are so eager to prove impersonal will prove to be personal, and will also appear then more terrible and more pitiful even than it does now" – a wonderfully prophetic remark.

In 1948 Berryman began writing his masterwork, "Homage to Mistress Bradstreet," which was to preoccupy him for the next five years. In his account of his – and Eileen's – agonies in composing this work, Mr. Mariani almost justifies his biography by going into detail about a period which Mr. Haffenden has scanted. Those familiar with this long poem cannot forget the weird, near-pathological way in which Berryman injects the poet – himself – into the account of the life of this conventional woman, long and happily married and 300 years dead, as her would-be lover. His biographer, seemingly infected with Berryman's weirdness, says that Berryman, having fallen in love with his creation, "meant to seduce it too. Anne, though tempted by his advances, would at last reject him, for which 'betrayal' she would be made to die slowly and painfully."

Six pages later, Mr. Mariani comments: "The inward fire of passion she had so long harbored Berryman would allow to consume her for having refused him." (Unfortunately, the beautiful quotes from Berryman and his friends a few pages earlier tend to make Mr. Mariani's prose even more grating than it would be otherwise.) I think we may take it that Mistress Bradstreet is a projection of Berryman's ambivalent feelings about his wife, his mother, his mistresses and of course himself – a not unusual mix for a poet.

With the completion of "Bradstreet" in 1953, Berryman's first marriage was also finished. Two years later he was hard at work on his astounding "Dream Songs." A brief second marriage (1956–59), to Elizabeth Ann Levine, produced a son, Paul. Through all these years his drinking became more and more a problem. His idea of moderation was a quart of whisky a day and four packs of Tareytons. During a few months he spent at Berkeley in 1960, he was drinking so much that he wet the bed. This is a sample of the edifying information that Mr. Mariani passes on, information that Mr. Haffenden mercifully withheld. A couple of drunken episodes witnessed by the poet W.S. Merwin are described in detail. Mr. Mariani might better have quoted from Mr. Merwin's poem "Berryman":

> . . . he was deep
> in tides of his own through which he sailed
> chin sideways and head tilted like a tacking sloop . . .
> as for publishing he advised me
> to paper my walls with rejection slips
> his lips and the bones of his long fingers trembled
> with the vehemence of his views about poetry
> he said the great presence
> that permitted everything and transmuted it
> in poetry was passion
> passion was genius and he praised movement and invention.

For the rest of the biography, Mr. Mariani spares neither the reader nor Berryman, his children, wives and friends. We are dragged relentlessly through every episode of mania, alcoholism and adultery – it is what a friend of mind has named "binge-by-binge biography." We learn, of course, of Berryman's third marriage in 1961, to Kathleen Ann Donahue, and the births of his two daughters. We are informed of the genesis of some of the "Dream Songs" (*77 Dream Songs,* published by Farrar, Straus, in 1964, won the Pulitzer Prize). Prizes and binges alternated with increasing frenzy. In 1970 Berryman experienced what he felt was "a sort of religious conversion": a shift from a belief in a transcendent God, a formal principle holding the universe together, to a God who cared for our individual fates. He then wrote his "Eleven Addresses to the Lord." The sixth begins:

> Under new management, Your Majesty:
> Thine. I have solo'd mine since childhood, since
> my father's suicide when I was twelve
> blew out my most bright candle faith, and look at me . . .
>
> My double nature fused in that point of time
> three weeks ago day before yesterday.
> Now, brooding thro' a history of the early Church,
> I identify with everybody, even the heresiarchs.

When this appeared in a book of poems, "Love & Fame," Hayden Carruth was infuriated because of its precise dating of Berryman's revelation. Mr. Carruth refused to believe this "boasting, equivocating secularist" when he reviewed the book in *The Nation*. John's answer was that he had localized his religious experience in the way a lover "memorializes the date and place of his first kiss." I believe you, John, your last gasp for help, as you tried and failed Alcoholics Anonymous, then leaped from the bridge in Minneapolis in January 1972. *Pax vobiscum.*

KARL SHAPIRO

THE LIVES OF AMERICAN POETS are hazardous to their health. Succeed too late and you become bitter and cranky, like the late Robert Frost, who was recognized in America only after age forty. Succeed too soon and, like a football star, you continue to live in the memory of your glory days, besides running a serious risk of ending up a cripple.

Karl Shapiro was a success from the start of his career, when his work was published in 1941, the same year that he was drafted into the United States Army. He was twenty-eight. Over the next five years, he won virtually every prize worth having, culminating in the Pulitzer in 1945.

When he was released from the Army the following year, he immediately became Consultant in Poetry at the Library of Congress – the youngest poet ever to achieve this distinction (now called the Poet Laureateship). The book under review *Reports of My Death* (Algonquin Books, 1990) is the second volume of Shapiro's autobiography, and dramatically illustrates the price he paid for early success.

In the first volume, *The Younger Son,* Shapiro, referring to himself in the third person, says, "He wasn't ready to be memorialized; he was only experimenting, he hadn't even started. To be put on a pedestal before your clay was dry was to invite disaster."

The curious thing about Shapiro is that he not only invited disaster, he lusted after it, and, like blinded Samson, managed to pull down his temple of fame until it lay in ruins at his feet. And all too human, he spends a great many words in the present book kvetching about the neglect which, in large measure, he brought upon himself.

Part One of the present book begins in 1945. The poet has won the Pulitzer – which he calls The Golden Albatross – and his young wife, who mailed out his poems for him and dealt with his literary business while he was in the army, has had a baby, the first of three.

We get the prime whiff of Shapiro's free-floating paranoia when he says that the Library of Congress has the goods on him from the F B I. All his life he wonders if he shouldn't have joined the C I A and "could see himself lying dead in a ditch in Yugoslavia." Later on, when he attends the Salzburg Seminar, he tells us in all seriousness that he avoided Vienna because "he was afraid of being kidnapped by the Russians." God knows what we are to make of all this.

Shapiro's purely literary paranoia shows up early as well. He believes that "the critics, the real ones, were at this point arming themselves to the teeth and were on the verge of capturing the kingdom of poetry itself in a kind of fascist *coup d'état*." This passage neatly encapsulates a number of his obsessions, and also displays the intemperate generalizing and scatter-gun polemics which have contributed so heavily to damaging his reputation. He himself calls it "mad dog criticism" and can't comprehend why he should be shunned because of it. The natural impulse when you see someone foaming at the mouth is to run away, is it not? But Shapiro felt, and feels, that it is necessary for the poet "to engage in the critical battle because the world of poetry was in flames . . . In fact, he wanted to use [criticism] the way boys like to handle guns."

Shapiro is virtually alone among poets of his time in engaging in what might equally well be called macho criticism. The rest of us have just gone on writing our poems, perhaps the occasional essay, and paying little heed, if any, to the canons of academic criticism. Above all, we avoid making manifestos declaring that poetry has been shot down in flames because it only makes us look as if we had shot ourselves in the foot.

Despite – and sometimes because of – the rant quoted above, Shapiro is fun to read. His command of English, in both poetry and prose, is always impressive. His frankness is disarming. He professes to loathe confessional poetry, but he adores confessional prose, especially his own.

His adulteries seem obligatory, his home life a pain: "Home has already turned into a hell in the little apartment with two babies . . ."

The fuss at the Library of Congress over the awarding of the Bollingen Prize to Ezra Pound must have made a break in the monotony of baby screams. The former consultants at the Library of Congress, now named Fellows, formed a committee, with T.S. Eliot as Honorary Fellow, to bestow an award jointly by the Library of Congress and the Bollingen Foundation. (The award of the prize to Ezra Pound, then in St. Elizabeth's Hospital under a charge of treason for having broadcast for Mussolini during World War II, effectually stopped government support of the arts for twenty years.) Shapiro, as he himself admits, first said yes to Pound's award, then said no. But he believed that the Bollingen case followed him for the rest of his life – "the Jew who wouldn't let it rest . . . that broke his equanimity for good."

Eliot, "the spider," "the ghoul," "the walking cadaver," controlled the committee, he thought. Auden voted for Pound because he had been hurt by his Jewish lover; Robert Lowell was "sneering and shifty-eyed and sycophantic." No one, it seems, voted their convictions that Pound's work had value. Shapiro felt that the doors of the Establishment slammed on him forever. The fact that he has gone on flinging insults at everyone within range for the past forty years has had nothing to do with it, of course.

Shapiro shook the book dust of the Library of Congress from his feet and moved on to Johns Hopkins University. He didn't like it there either, and left to edit *Poetry* magazine in Chicago.

To illustrate the problem of referring to himself always in the third person, and his refusal to name virtually everyone else he encounters, check this passage: "Well, he discovered, the other editor had been manipulated, ideologically, as it were, by one or more of the New Critics, especially the Southerner poet-critic who had given the Consultantship job . . . to the poet editor-elect, and who was T.S. Eliot's right-hand man . . . " (If you're interested in untangling this mess, the Southern poet-critic and Eliot admirer was Allen Tate.)

I found it particularly irritating that Shapiro continually refers to the late Isabella Gardner as "a red-haired Boston Brahmin." Isabella Gardner was a fine poet, as Shapiro admits; she "slaved at the manuscripts [at *Poetry*] six hours a day for years even after he left . . . " and "they were lifelong friends."

What excuse does he have for omitting the name of one whose generosity was legend, and who gave so unstintingly to poetry and poets? Was it so that he could drag in a mention of "her many lovers, one of whom was a black man who broke her arm and put her in the hospital"? You would be even angrier at Shapiro if he didn't so often apply the same brutal treatment to himself.

Taking time off from *Poetry* to attend the Salzburg Seminar, Shapiro became more and more reclusive and took to hiding out in his room. Like a *rosé*, Shapiro has never travelled well. In Paris, on the way home, he goes to the Louvre and looks at the *Mona Lisa* (who resembles a postage stamp), visits Saint-Sulpice and "the enormous Delacroix in the dark church, some massacre or other . . . " "In such a city he had nothing to do . . . " I wonder if instead of adopting Theodore Roethke's name for him, "The Bourgeois Poet," he shouldn't have called himself "The Parochial Poet."

Shapiro then taught part-time at Iowa, a job he quit in midstream. He quit *Poetry* magazine. "The way he shed jobs, like a poodle shaking off bath water, astonished his friends." And all for a semester at Berkeley, which he adored, but unfortunately the feeling was not mutual. After a State Department-sponsored trip to India which was aborted for some mysterious reason (though at this point the attentive reader can guess why), he went to the University of Nebraska and the editorship of *Prairie Schooner.*

The reader is now launched into Part Two, where she or he may learn of Shapiro's flirtation with the Beat poets and Zen, all of which will turn sour in the sixties, when Shapiro has a violent reaction to the student revolution and all that accompanied it.

They will learn that his obstinate perversity even extends to a defense of airline food! They will learn how he screwed up his Guggenheim in Italy and had to come home with wife, children and station wagon after a couple of months because he hated his eighteenth century villa, his offspring howled for hamburgers, and he had been unable to keep track of his finances – a customary failing of his in which he seems to take undue pride.

Back in Nebraska, his marriage falls apart, he finds himself more and more attracted to sexual obscenity and the likes of Henry Miller. For a fuller account of this period, especially of sexual perversity in Lincoln, Neb., the reader may consult Shapiro's scabrous novel, *Edsel,* so aptly named, in which he makes only half-hearted attempts at concealing its autobiographical content.

In the novel, he calls the woman he takes up with while both are undergoing divorce "Marya." She relieves him of both his physical and literary impotence. In "Reports of My Death," he continues to call the woman who became his second wife "Marya." Her name was Teri Kovach, a lovely, warm, blooming woman whom all his friends loved. Again, to make anonymous the good and kindly women who lightened his life seems a kind of literary mayhem, to say the least. But in truth there is only one character in Shapiro's life, one figure that we see with vividness and clarity: Shapiro himself.

In Part Three of his autobiography, also called *Reports of My Death,* he reveals his wounded feelings at being treated as if he no longer existed. He begins to notice that "the newer anthologies were beginning to drop him from what had been a standard roster of poets of his age."

The unkindest cut was from *The Oxford Book of American Verse,* after fifteen editions and twenty-five years. But from his earliest criticism to the present volume Shapiro has insisted that American poetry was "sick," "maimed," "crumbling under the pressures of criticism," "murdered," indeed "dead." Did Shapiro then expect his colleagues to rush up and thank him for saying that their life's work was a bootless enterprise and their own work worthless, and smother him with kisses? One can't help believing that these repeated asseverations are part of his own literary death-wish.

By a series of episodes too complicated to go into here, including the death of his second wife, and a paper in a medical journal listing literary suicides which includes Shapiro's name, he is indeed left for dead in the *Saturday Evening Post;* in the *New York Times* crossword puzzle, the answer to *thirteen* across: "late U.S. Poet," is Shapiro. Of course this is sad and unfair, but feisty Shapiro, happily remarried, will stay in there punching, we can be sure.

Perhaps the best way to sum up is to quote Shapiro on Ezra Pound: "And yet under it all one feels a flow of sympathy, a kindliness and a sorrow for [him]. He is such a storybook American, a stereotype, and a scapegoat certainly. And when you come right down to it, there is something lovable about the old man."

ROBERT CREELEY

READER, ARE YOU OLD ENOUGH to remember the excitement commingled with joy, in which in the early sixties we fell upon a whole run of poems collected in a volume called *For Love* (Scribner, 1962)? Poems that became famous almost overnight, and that you of subsequent generations may have discovered in your own time, poems like "The Crisis" which begins:

> Let me say (in anger) that since the day we were married
> we have never had a towel
> where anyone could find it.

the fact
> Notwithstanding that I am not
simple to live with, not
my own judgement, but no
matter . . .

The first poem of his that I fell in love with was "After Lorca":

> The church is a business, and the rich
> are the business men.
> > When they pull on the bells, the
> poor come piling in and when a poor man dies, he has a
> wooden
> cross, and they rush through the ceremony.

> But when a rich man dies, they
> drag out the Sacrament
> and a golden Cross, and go *doucement, doucement*
> to the cemetery.

> And the poor love it
> and think it's crazy.

And the mock paranoia of the poet in "The Dishonest Mailmen," which rapidly modulates into real heroism, all in the space of ten lines:

> They are taking all my letters, and they
> put them into a fire.
> > I see the flames, etc.
> But do not care, etc.

> They burn everything I have, or what little
> I have. I don't care, etc.

> The poem supreme, addressed to
> emptiness—this is the courage

> necessary. This is something
> quite different.

The fine ironies at the beginning of "The Immoral Proposition":

> If you never do anything for anyone else
> you are spared the tragedy of human relation-
> ships...

The subtle music of "Chanson":

> Oh, le petit rondelay!
> Gently, gently.
> It is that I grow older.

It was not only the beautiful pacing of the thing, it was those line-breaks that got us: "moist-er," which is to grow more slowly moist; "in-clination" which so gently leans. Oh, that his imitators had his skills! But, *tristement, tristement,* they don't.

Then there is the intimate, confiding air of "The Conspiracy," where we're not just the reader over his shoulder but the recipient of the message:

> You send me your poems,
> I'll send you mine...
>
> Let us suddenly
> proclaim spring. And jeer
>
> at the others,
> all the others.
>
> I will send a picture too
> if you will send me one of you.

(I wonder how many sent pictures.)

Then perhaps his most famous poem, "I Know a Man."

> And I sd to my
> friend, because I am
> always talking, – John, I

sd, which was not his
name, the darkness sur-
rounds us, what

can we do against
it, or else, shall we &
why not, buy goddamn big car,

drive, he sd, for
christ's sake, look
out where yr going.

(Oh, that his followers could use his shorthand as he does! But really, they haven't earned the right; Creeley isn't, as many seem to think, in the public domain.) Here, in a couple of lines, he sums up the deep inner feelings of us Americans: the darkness surrounds us; let's buy a big car. Only Louis Simpson has come so close to encapsulating our true nature.

"My enemies came to get me, / among them a beautiful woman," Creeley begins in "A Form of Adaptation." "They are wise to send their strongest first, I thought. / And I kissed her." It ends:

And they watched her and both of us carefully,
not at all to be tricked.

But how account for love, even if you look for it?
I trusted it.

Here we come to Creeley's most plangent theme: the varieties of love, and the varieties of response to it. He has been foolishly called "a domestic poet" (probably the only male poet to have that label hung on him, though it's common to tag us female poets with it, though we write of Bach, the Wobblies and the Unified Field Theory); "the poet of intimacies" would be more like it.

. . . the Lady is indefinable,
she will be the door in the wall

> to the garden in sunlight.
> I will go on talking forever.
>
> I will never get there.
> Oh Lady, remember me
> who in Your service grows older
> not wiser, no more than before.

This is part of one of the noble poems to the Muse ("The Lady has always moved to the next town / and you stumble on after Her"), called "The Door." It ends:

> . . . I will go to the garden.
> I will be a romantic. I will sell
> myself in hell,
> in heaven also I will be.
>
> In my mind I see the door,
> I see the sunlight before me across the floor
> beckon to me, as the Lady's skirt
> moves small beyond it.

He is able, quite unself-consciously, to be intimate on great and sacred matters. He found his voice, early on, and a more characteristic aspect of his genius is the way he gives substance to ephemeral events: the events, which, in accretion, make up our lives. But for years critics have bedevilled themselves, and us, in their attempts to "place" Creeley; the old rating game: is he major or minor? has he gone from strength to strength, or withered away? Periodically, some critic has announced that Creeley was becoming so minimal that he was in danger of disappearing altogether. So, in the 1970s, he wrote a series of magnificent longer poems, including the elegy to his mother, Genevieve Jules Creeley, of whom he had already written memorably ("Mother was helpful but essentially mistaken. / It is the second half of the 20th century / I screamed . . .").

The obsession to rank and rate poets, to confer greatness by comparison, is always with us. Fortunately we readers – you and I – are the true judge and jury, because our criteria is pleasure and enlightenment, not

exegesis and paraphrasis. Like Hart Crane, whom he revers and refers
to, Creeley is not placeable in ways reassuring to the academic mind.
His inwardness, elusiveness, his near-secretiveness (except that ordinary mortals are let in on the secrets if we care enough) resist the cata-
logue. For most of his fifty-seven years he has known who he is and
what he is. That is not a secret. It should be enough, and it is.

Let me close by quoting two passages from the poem to his mother:

> ... Walk
> a little, get
>
> up, now, die
> safely,
> easily, into
>
> singleness, too
> tired with it
> to keep
>
> on and on.
> Waves break at
> the darkness
>
> under the road, sounds
> in the faint
> night's softness. Look
>
> ... how
>
> long you kept
> at it, your
> pride, your
>
> lovely, confusing
> discretion. Mother, I
> love you—for
>
> whatever that
> means ...

Lovely confusing discretion – how characteristic of Creeley that phrase is! "One of the most lovely insistences in Whitman's poems" (from an essay); "I like to drink / and talk to people, / all the lovely faces" (from "Dear Dorothy"); "Your face passes down the street – / your hair that was so lovely / your body, won't wait for me" (from "Flesh") – and the word occurs again and again in letters, essays and dedications. What other (male) poet can take these chances?

In the introduction to *The Collected Poems of Robert Creeley, 1945–1975* (University of California Press, 1982), Creeley says, "There is sense of increment, of accumulation, in these poems that is very dear to me . . . when it came time to think specifically of this collection and of what might be decorously omitted I decided to stick with my initial judgement, book by tender book . . . " Dear, lovely, decorous, tender – ah, there is no one like him! Thank you, Bob.

GARY SNYDER

IN 1955, FRESH FROM HIS TRIUMPH at the Six Gallery in San Francisco where he recited "Howl" to a stunned audience for the first time, Allen Ginsberg showed up with his cohort, Gary Snyder, to read their poems at the University of Washington. They were dressed identically in black turtlenecks and jeans, with "Ez for Prez" buttons pinned to their sweaters (Ezra Pound, not Ezra Taft Benson, as the more conventional poet I was dating at the time observed sourly – Benson being the current secretary of agriculture under Eisenhower, not the famed poet who had been tried for treason). Ginsberg, fuzzy and hairy, read "Howl" to predictable gasps and a few walkouts. Snyder, fresh-faced, red-headed and neatly put together (as he still is), read a few poems in traditional meters (some of which can be found in the eighth section of *No Nature: New and Selected Poems* (Pantheon, 1992), then announced dramatically, "Enough of this Yeatsean Eliotic stuff!" and launched into a few of the poems that are still characteristic of his work today: fresh, minutely observed evocations of the world of nature in which he had immersed himself, in free meters. Gary was twenty-five.

A dozen years later, my young daughter was an exchange student in Japan. On a field trip, without a syllable of preparation, she was herded into the Hiroshima Museum. The horror and shock of what she saw sent her fleeing from the museum, back on the train to Tokyo. She was huddled on a bench, weeping, when an attractive, kindly young red-headed man came down the aisle and tried to comfort the girl. Being a well-read child, she recognized his name when he mentioned it, and said shyly that her mother was a poet too. On hearing my name – far more obscure than his own – he at once embraced her.

In the middle of the next decade, Gary Snyder and John Hollander and I were sitting in the handsome office of the Consultant in Poetry at the Library of Congress. Two poets more unlike could hardly be imagined: Hollander, formalist, academic, rather stuffy and shy, the archetypal Inside Man confronting Gary, the inimitable Outside Man, ardent and poised. How did they get along? Famously. Both men are etymology freaks; arcane word derivations were flying around the room like paper airplanes, buzzed by phrases from half a dozen arcane languages. They had such a good time! Stanley Kunitz, the poetry consultant, and I turned from one man to the other as if we were watching a particularly inspired badminton match between two champions.

Interviewed during the seventies, Snyder said that poetry comes to him from the outside, not from the inside. In a new poem, "How Poetry Comes to Me," near the end of *No Nature,* he writes:

> It comes blundering over the
> Boulders at night, it stays
> Frightened outside the
> Range of my campfire
> I go to meet it at the
> Edge of the light

This is what Snyder, the greatest of living nature poets, means by calling his book "No Nature." In the preface he writes: "The greatest respect we can pay to nature is not to trap it, but to acknowledge that it eludes us and that our own nature is also fluid, open, and conditional." The last poem in the book echoes the phrase, implying that to set any limits on nature is to deny its essence. Nature is everywhere, within and without, in, as he says in another poem, "parsnips or diapers, the deathless / nobility at the core of all ordinary things," and in Shakespeare and Li Po, the good, bedrock ordinariness in the mind of genius.

The first poem in the book, from *Riprap* (1959), "Mid-August at Sourdough Mountain Lookout," reveals how early Snyder found his own voice, and with what sureness he set down the lines:

> Down valley a smoke haze
> Three days heat, after five days rain
> Pitch glows on the fir-cones
> Across rocks and meadows
> Swarms of new flies.
>
> I cannot remember things I once read
> A few friends, but they are in cities.
> Drinking cold snow-water from a tin cup
> Looking down for miles
> Through high still air.

Not yet thirty when he wrote this, he incorporated so many of the elements we still recognize in his work: the quality that the first stanza shares with Sung landscape painting; the first couplet in the second stanza reminiscent of the T'ang poet, Po Chu-I; some of the five senses in the last three lines – taste, touch and sight. And we taste the cold metal of that cup with our lips and teeth – that snow-cold water!

But several aspects of Snyder's work emerge in this collection that haven't, to my knowledge, been recognized. For example, reviewers and interviewers customarily bring up the Oriental and Zen elements in Snyder's work. They tend to overlook the quite open references to Western literature. Often these references are made lightheartedly and playfully, as in "Milton by Fire-Light," in which the central figure proclaims: "O hell, what do mine eyes with grief behold?" and proceeds to question the relevance of these lines while he's blasting granite with an old single-jack miner. He goes on to say that the Sierras will be dead in ten thousand years, "No paradise, no fall. . . . Oh Hell!" The poem ends sweetly:

> The bell-mare clangs in the meadow
> That packed dirt for a fill-in
> Scrambling through loose rocks
> On an old trail
> All of the summer's day.

That last line, as if to tease Milton's orotund rhetoric, is from a simple old nursery rhyme (the line itself copied and teased by Lewis Carroll as well).

In a series of poems called "Logging," from *Myths and Texts* (New Directions, 1978), writing of a pine cone chased by squirrels, Snyder quotes Keats: "What mad pursuit! What struggle to escape!" again playfully; these poems contain references to Han Shan, Crazy Horse, the Gautama, the Haida, Cybele and the Weyerhaeuser Timber Company. And, to quote from his cohort, Robert Creeley, "They all fit!" because Snyder has so fully internalized everything he has ever seen.

Eroticism is another quality frequently overlooked in Snyder's poetry. Take the poem "Night," from *The Back Country* (New Directions, 1968)

> . . . the bit tongue and trembling ankle,
> joined palms and twined legs,
> the tilted chin and beat cry,
> hunched shoulders and a throb in the belly.
> teeth swim in loose tongues, with toes curled.
> eyes snapped shut, and quick breath.
> hair all tangled together.

There are others—"September," "Beneath My Hand and Eye the Distant Hills, Your Body"—in which the account of lovemaking is equally vivid and poignant because it occurs in the midst of homely, ordinary things: "ate dinner on worn mats / clean starcht yukata / warm whisky with warm water . . . told each other / what we'd never said before, ah, / dallying on mats / whispering sweat / cools our kissing skin. . . ."

Poems like "Axe Handles" (from the book of the same name) are much more basic to the Snyder cosmos. In this poem, Snyder is teaching his son, Kai, to make a hatchet by carving an old axe handle into a hatchet handle. He is reminded of a phrase first learned from Ezra Pound, which is a translation from the "Wen Fu" of Lu Ji, a fourth century discourse on poetics: "In making the handle of an axe by cutting wood with an axe the model is indeed near at hand."

> My teacher Shih-hsiang Chen
> Translated that and taught it years ago
> And I see: Pound was an axe,
> Chen was an axe, I am an axe
> And my son a handle, soon
> To be shaping again, model
> And tool, craft of culture,
> How we go on.

How we go on. . . . And it helps us to go on, having Gary Snyder in our midst.

Others Call it God:
Hayden Carruth

In the early sixties, when I was editing *Poetry Northwest*, I received a group of poems from Hayden Carruth, including a sonnet called, "Ontological Episode of the Asylum." Although I had read a number of his poems and some of his criticism with admiration, I did not know Carruth personally. But this group of poems was the beginning of a friendship which has remained steadfast ever since. The sonnet, in particular, moved me then – to the point where I almost instantly memorized it – and moves me now, not only because the form is perfectly subsumed in the subject but because it summed up my own feelings about belief:

> The boobyhatch's bars, the guards, the nurses,
> The illimitable locks and keys are all arranged
> To thwart the hand that continually rehearses
> Its ending stroke and raise a barricade
> Against destruction-seeking resolution.
> Many of us in there would have given all
> (But we had nothing) for one small razor blade
> Or seventy grams of the comforting amytal.
>
> So I went down in the attitude of prayer,
> Yes, to my knees on the cold floor of my cell,
> Humped in a corner, a bird with a broken wing,
> And asked and asked as fervently and well
> As I could guess to do for light in the mists
> Of death, until I learned God doesn't care.

> Not only that, he doesn't care at all,
> One way or the other. That is why he exists.

I am surely not the only person to be reminded of the famous passage in William James's *The Varieties of Religious Experience,* where he speaks in the guise of a Frenchman "in a bad nervous condition." Later, he confessed that this had been his own experience:

> While in this state of philosophic pessimism and general depression of spirits about my prospects, I went one evening into a dressing-room in the twilight to procure some article that was there; when suddenly there fell upon me without warning, just as if it came out of the darkness, a horrible fear of my own existence. Simultaneously there arose in my mind the image of an epileptic patient whom I had seen in the asylum, a black-haired youth with greenish skin, entirely idiotic, who used to sit all day on one of the benches, or rather shelves against the wall, with his knees drawn up against his chin . . . This image and my fear entered into a species of combination with each other. *That shape am I,* I felt, potentially. Nothing that I possess can defend me against that fate, if the hour for it should strike for me as it struck for him . . . I have always thought that this experience of melancholia of mine had a religious bearing."

On responding to a question of himself by himself, James added, "I mean that the fear was so invasive and powerful that if I had not clung to scripture – texts like 'The eternal God is my refuge' etc., 'Come unto me, all ye that labor and are heavy laden,' etc., I think I should have grown really insane."

Of course calling on God in extremis is not unique to poets and philosophers, but to pray without any expectation of being heard or being helped is perhaps more unusual. It could even be considered an act of heroism, as indeed Carruth calls it in another poem, "Once and Again," written more than a dozen years later, in a situation similar to that of the sonnet:

> . . . To believe in the God
> who does not exist is a heroism of faith, much needed in these
>   times,

> I agree, I know, especially since the hero is and must always be
> unrecognized. But to love the God that does not exist, to love
>   the love
> that does not exist, this is more than heroism, it is perhaps
>   almost
> saintliness, such as we can know it. To discover and to hold, to
>   resurrect
> an idea for its own sake . . .

To me, Carruth exaggerates the element of heroism and "perhaps almost saintliness" in this gratuitous love of God, and underestimates the
neurotic/creative act of the imagination which makes it possible. Elsewhere in *The Varieties of Religious Experience,* James makes the point
that, "Few of us are not in some ways infirm, or even diseased; and our
very infirmities help us unexpectedly." "If there were such a thing as inspiration from a higher realm, it might well be that the neurotic tem-
perament would furnish the chief condition of the requisite receptivity." From the pit of our desperation we call out to God, even if we
don't believe in him, and in the state of receptivity engendered by fear,
particularly fear of the cosmos, we may even dream of a response, although not a personal one, and not a comforting one. The sole comfort
comes from the act of prayer itself.

Later, James quotes Sabatier, the "liberal French theologian," perhaps the inspiration for James's imaginary Frenchman, in regard to
prayer: "Religion is nothing if it be not the vital act by which the entire
mind seeks to save itself by clinging to the principle from which it
draws its life. This act is prayer, by which term I understand no vain exercise of words, no mere repetition of certain sacred formulae, but the
very movement itself of the soul . . . Wherever the interior prayer is
lacking, there is no religion; wherever, on the other hand, the prayer
rises and stirs the soul, even in the absence of forms or doctrines, we
have living religion." Sabatier, however, would not agree with Carruth
because he believed that prayer was a placing of one's self into a personal relation with a mysterious power, while the prayers of unbeliev-
ing believers go out to an indifferent God, a God who may not exist at
all except as we pray to It.

At the end of his book, James remarks that the God whom science recognizes "must be a God of universal laws exclusively, a God who does a wholesale, not a retail business. He cannot accommodate his processes to the convenience of individuals." "Convenience" is perhaps too casual a word to describe the emotions of those who, in primal panic, fall on their knees in the desperate hope that God will respond and save. Carruth is harsh in his response to John Berryman's late conversion to belief in a personal God, Berryman, too, an alcoholic and – to use Carruth's own word about himself – "crazy." For most of his life Berryman had believed in a transcendent God – "a formal principle of sorts holding the vast complicated harmony of the universe together." This view is rather like the speculative theology of Empedocles, who spoke of God as "a sacred and unutterable mind, flashing through the whole world with rapid thought." Near his end, in the sixth of his "Eleven Addresses to the Lord," Berryman began:

> Under new management, Your Majesty:
> Thine. I have solo'd mine since childhood, since
> my father's suicide when I was twelve
> blew out my most bright candle faith, and look at me . . .
>
> My double nature fused in that point of time
> three weeks ago day before yesterday.
> Now, brooding thro' a history of the early Church
> I identify with everybody, even the heresiarchs.

Carruth was infuriated with the precise dating of Berryman's revelation, and refused to believe "this boasting, equivocating secularist," when he reviewed *Love & Fame* in *The Nation*. (Are we least sympathetic with those who share some of our darkest failings?)

Perhaps we might agree with one of James's critics who said that "his need to believe was tantamount to having faith" (but this is an attempt to clarify what James deliberately chose to keep obscure). Or, if we cannot agree, we may at least sympathize with those who feel that, in order to stave off insanity, they require some form of belief. Carruth goes out of his way to deny his own belief, but all the same he turns to God when he is "crazy" and only then.

The following appears in excerpts from *The Bloomingdale Papers*

(University of Georgia Press, 1975), his poems of the asylum, published after the fact, in 1975:

NOTE: Most inmates believe the alcoholics have the easiest portion; neither their illness nor their treatment seems particularly uncomfortable, even though the percentage of permanent cures is low—a little sodium amytal and some vitamin shots during the first days in the hatch are usually enough to straighten them out. The alcoholics themselves believe this and hold themselves somewhat aloof from the rest of us, who are crazy. [It must have been somewhat later that Carruth admitted to himself that he too was an alcoholic.]

*   *   *

Save me, O God; for the waters are come in
    unto my soul.

I sink in deep mire, where there is no standing:
I am come into deep waters, where the floods
    overflow me.
I am weary of my crying: my throat is dried:
    mine eyes fail . . .

Deliver me out of the mire, and let me not sink:
let me be delivered from them that hate me,
and out of the deep waters.

Let not the waterflood overflow me, neither
    let the deep swallow me up,
    and let not the pit
    shut her mouth upon me.

In a review in *Harper's* in 1976, Carruth says that "the answer to grief is God, but God does not answer." What then are we to make of his denial of belief coupled with his cries to cold heaven?

In an essay called "Who I Am, 1" he says, speaking of critics, that "they will not consider the work of art as *a transaction between the artist's soul and God*—substitute whatever other two words you like. But that's what it is." (My italics.) I think we must focus on the artist negotiating with his angel—his muse—rather than simply as a man pleading with God, as in the chant of the psalmist quoted above.

In another essay called "The Act of Love: Poetry and Personality," also published in 1976, Carruth restates a position he had taken earlier, in an essay on Robert Lowell: "The poet," he says, "was engaged in the conversion of crude experience into personality through metaphor and the other disciplines of the instrumental imagination," using the term "personality" to mean "the whole individual subjectivity, the spirit-body-soul."

I'm not entirely happy with Carruth's use of the term personality (in fact when I first typed the title of this article I Freudianly left off half of it: Poetry and Personality). Of course we are in semantic difficulties, as is almost invariably the case when attempting to talk of matters spiritual and metaphysical. There is no dictionary definition of personality which includes the entity spirit-body-soul, but it's a question of who is master here, and in this case we must concede that Carruth is. But he does seem to leave out a vital step, *the* vital step of the process, which is the conversion of crude experience into the final product, which is art. I find that a great deal of the poetry being written today is hung up on precisely that hook: personality, whether interpreted narrowly or in the broadest sense; and that the act of transcendence never takes place because the personality intervenes.

But let us go along with Carruth as he expands his definition: He says, further, that personality is universal and relative; it exists in every consciousness. "Personality is a phenomenon of pure existence and occurs in what have been called our existential moments, our moments outside time." The existential moment for the poet occurs when she or he is "intensely engaged in a poem, spontaneously engendering imagery and verbal compounds from the imaginative structures of remembered experience . . . It is a spiritual happening – at least I do not know what else to call it." Nor do I.

Carruth asserts again that he is not a religious person. He cannot "project this concept of spirit and personality onto any traditional religion that I know, although analogues and affinities occur in many of them." Further, he says that he uses the word "spiritual" to mean "the substance of feeling when personality passes out of time's determinants and into pure essence, which I have called eternity; and in poems I have spoken of meetings there with the holy spirit, though my meaning has not been the same one that Christians use when they refer to the third attribute of the Trinity." "Chiefly I think of the transcendence of personality as a process of innerness, and of the holy spirit as my own." (My own preference would be to use "identity," even spiritual identity, rather than personality. Moreover, I don't see how Carruth can call the holy spirit "my own" when he has supposedly transcended his personality.)

But by now I believe that we have circled back to where we started: with Carruth's poems. In his shying away from the thought that he is a religious man, or a man who can relate to a form of traditional religion, he is in a sense contradicting his own poems, which seem to tell a different story. How many of these defiant rejections of any whiff of traditional faith might have been rendered unnecessary – and conserving of psychic energy – if we, like the American Indians before us, believed in and called upon The Great Spirit, rather than God!

Poetry is not prayer, but it is not not prayer. Prayer is not often poetry, but the greatest prayers are poems. To me, the spiritual is the spiritual, no matter how we quibble over terminology, qualify it or attempt to redefine it. Spirituality is identical with, and achieved through, an act of love. Carruth says as much at the close of his essay: "What I have in mind is what has been called in other places the 'aesthetic emotion,' the feeling that overlies substance and converts substance, whether beautiful or ugly, into something else. Sometimes this 'something else' has been called beauty, but the term is likely to be misunderstood" (like all the other terms we have been using). "I prefer to call it spiritual love, the state of being of a pure existence, and the aesthetic emotion is the experience of that state."

However, none of these aesthetic impulses, no matter what their degree of spirituality, can succeed in warding off that cosmic fear. When, in the night, it overtakes us, we turn instinctively to prayer, to the great spirit who is within us. As for me, I pray a good deal, even when I'm not scared or miserable. And one of the people I pray for, nearly every day, is my dear friend, Hayden Carruth. God may not listen or care, one way or the other. But It exists.

Wrapped in Silk:
Marie Ponsot

Ice thaws in a poet's throat; the springing
truth is fresh. It wakes taste.   The taste lasts.
Language floods the mud; mind makes a cast of words;
it precipitates, like silvery T'ang discourse
riding the tidal constant of its source.

As I say these lines to myself, an old memory rises to the surface:
Hangchow, the poets' lake, which I saw as a girl, and see as clearly in
my mind today. It is a symbol of all that is calm, graceful, elegant, en-
during in the poet-life; the same can be said of these words by Marie
Ponsot. Perhaps fame never happens, or it comes and just as suddenly
vanishes, and may recur after death. Never mind. The lines live. The
lake goes on for another thousand years, though in English its spelling
changes to the harsh and difficult *Hangzhou* in the title of Marie's
poem.

   The first section of her new book, *The Green Dark* (Alfred A. Knopf,
1988) is called "The Story of the Problems." One favorite of mine is
called "The Problem of the Experimental Method," which begins,

Today she learns that up is marvelous.
Water rises up unseen, falls, and appears
as crystals, their difference too sharp for us
to see without a magnifying glass
or save, or savor . . .

and ends,

> . . . Experiments don't take her far.
> Words do, without policing. Words keep here, here.
> Their gravity homes her, on her native star.

For me, the opening is sweetly reminiscent of Louise Bogan's "Roman Fountain":

> Up from the bronze, I saw
> Water without a flaw
> Rush to its rest in air,
> Reach to its rest, and fall . . .

And the Bogan analogy holds in more ways than that. There is the absolute control of language, the seeming effortlessness (grown out of who knows how many nights of pondering, sighs, and rewriting), the chiming of words: "see . . . save . . . savor," "rush . . . reach . . . rest"; the canny use of rhyme and off-rhyme — though Bogan's skill is such that the poem occasionally says to you, "Look at me!" Ponsot's forms rarely call attention to themselves. It is this modesty of hers, so prized by her peers, that has perhaps limited her reputation among general readers.

"The Problem of Outside In" begins,

> Big trees make
> the east field dark first. A shadowy
> rabbit emerges. Shadowy grasses shake.
>
> The archaic red-gold
> that washes far slopes in one gold-red
> rims tree-crowns in the west hill-fold.

(Oh, it's painful not to quote her poems in full, so all of a piece they are!) That splendid opening parade of monosyllables; those daring sibilants; those splendid spondees, five in three lines! We are in the hands of a mistress of her craft. It is a curious little irony that these poems are called "Problems," when for the reader there is no problem at all; we are nested in down and wrapped in silk.

You probably can't be this skillful without being witty as well. Take "The Royal Gate," for example:

> Little Jacqueline Pascal played with Blaise
> reinventing Euclid (Papa told them to).
> While he made up conic sections, she wrote plays
> & got papa out of jail when Richelieu
> liked her long impromptu poem in his praise.

And there is an extremely funny, witty poem called "Defusing The Usual Criminal Metaphors," which describes the pathos of the penis, as opposed to the hardened fantasies of Hemingways, pornographers and such. I won't quote it. I want you women out there to buy the book!

At present, I believe my favorite poem is a longer piece called "Spring Song." (As we all know, our favorites shift, depending on our moods and seasons; also, with Marie Ponsot, as thoroughly grown-up as any writer living, some of us have some growing-up to do in order to fathom all of her.) I love not only the poem itself but its theme: friendship. Once I was on a panel with the distinguished George Steiner, when I remarked that part of my attraction to Chinese poetry of the classical period (I see that this review is going to be circular: ending as it began, with the T'ang Dynasty) was that its chief subject was friendship. George, who is no man to mince words, replied, "Nonsense!" and proceeded to cite some great poems in the English tradition. To which I replied, "Yes, George, but all the friends to whom those poems were written were dead." Well, Marie has, with this poem, done a great deal to make up for these deficiencies in our tradition. I'll quote three passages:

> Here are two solid bodies, wingless, bodies of friends
> who are never lovers, bare of former wife and
> former husband and usual circumstance.
> We are two bony poets horizontal under
> the wash of moon, its ennobling shadows.

*   *   *

Free to dream we do not haunt each other.
What I say when I talk in my sleep
I trust you with, so you may guess that across
my inner sky (as yours, I'd say)
the vertical longing soars.

We leave each other safe. I leave to dream
wings and wing-arms, wristed, hauling
the dark form, its bones full of air, in a surge
in a tube of whistling in a triumph otherwise
silent in unguessable flight, almost
making out in translation
the words of the celebrant
and the syllable it celebrates.

(from "Spring Song")

"Silvery T'ang discourse" indeed. And more – as we will never know
the exact sounds made by those five syllables to the line – music. I hope
you hear that music in your mind when I say that Marie Ponsot is the
Couperin of poets.

The Other Side of the Story: Sylvia Plath

F RANKLY, I'M FED UP with the endless probings of the lives
of lady poets who have suicided themselves. I'd prefer to read about
survivors, like Adrienne Rich or Denise Levertov, poets now in their
sixties who are even better than they were at thirty, the age at which
Sylvia Plath stuck her head in the oven.

I'd even be fed up with yet another piece on Anne Sexton, although
she was a friend of mine and a nice woman. Sylvia Plath was not a
friend of mine and not a nice woman. So I read *Bitter Fame: A Life of
Sylvia Plath* by Anne Stevenson (Houghton Mifflin, 1989) only because I'd been given it to review.

I surprised myself by liking it, for it is sensible, steady, decently written and a corrective to the wilder notions that have grown like weeds
over the years: for instance, that Plath, the girl genius, was trammelled
by matrimony and babies, and had a faithless husband who cruelly deserted her in her desperate hours, thus contributing to her early death.

This myth has been perpetrated in part by angry feminists, including
me, and is a large factor in Plath's posthumous fame. The fame and the
suicide have been so closely entwined that for a number of years
anxious young women writers would inquire of the likes of me if they
had to kill themselves to become famous.

Now in measured phrases Anne Stevenson lays out the kind of person who was Sylvia. A genius? Yes, if you're a sucker for what this author calls, "nerve-peeled surrealism" and "macabre doom-laden themes,
heavy with disturbing colors and totemlike images of stones, skulls,
drownings, snakes and bottled fetuses."

It turns out that Plath, far from being trammelled by marriage and two young children, loved domesticity, was an accomplished and happy cook, adored children and wanted more – although in her last days when her husband had left her and she felt herself coming apart, she was as desperate as any of us might have been for help in caring for them.

And what about the husband, Ted Hughes, as gifted as she, now poet laureate of England? Stevenson makes a convincing case that he was a much put-upon man. Indeed, given Plath's mercurial shifts of mood from the girlish, all-American, bobby-soxed housewife, bubbling with enthusiasm, to the unspeaking and unspeakable Gorgon whose eyes could stun you with their poisoned darts, most men would have checked out a great deal sooner than he. Her two-sided self is strikingly shown by comparing quotes from *Letters Home* (Houghton Mifflin, 1989) written to her mother, Aurelia, all sunshine and boastful ambition, with the hysterical doom-fraught entries in her journals of the same period.

This hysteria mixed fatally with pathological jealousy of Hughes and women he encountered in a casual way. A middle-aged BBC producer with "a lilting Irish voice" over the phone arranged to meet with Hughes to discuss a series of children's programs. When he didn't return as promptly as she expected, Sylvia gathered together all his works in progress, his play, poems, notebooks, even his precious edition of Shakespeare, and ripped them into tiny pieces. How could one writer do this to another – not an enemy but a passionately beloved spouse? But, remarkably, within three weeks Hughes was tenderly caring for her when she was hospitalized for the removal of her appendix.

Stevenson deals glancingly and charitably with that classic stage mother, Aurelia Plath. When Hughes was unfaithful – as most people become after being accused of it – she slides over the affair. She neglects to tell us that the lady with whom he was spending time when Plath killed herself also committed suicide later – which might convince some people that Hughes was a lady-killer in the strictest sense of the term. However, I'm inclined to accept her portrait of Hughes with the reservation that, in an author's note, Stevenson calls the book the product of a "three-year dialogue between the author and Olwyn Hughes," the poet's sister and always fierce defender.

It's not to denigrate Stevenson's achievement to tell you that the best part of the book is a memoir by Dido Merwin, ex-wife of the poet W.S. Merwin. She is bitchy and shrewd and highly entertaining. She describes Sylvia as a blend of Medea and Emily Post, which pretty well sums up the message of the whole book.

Growing Old Alive: Kenneth O. Hanson and Han Yü

WHEN THE DEFINITIVE anthology of three thousand years of Chinese poetry, *Sunflower Splendor* (Indiana University Press, 1975), appeared some years ago, the translations of Kenneth O. Hanson were singled out by the knowledgeable reviewers as particularly praiseworthy. This was due not only to their accuracy, but because they existed as poems in English, rather than—as seems largely inevitable in anthologies of this kind—academic paraphrases of the original poems, composed in that lingo never heard on the lips of man, known as "translatese." Those of us familiar with Hanson's earlier version of the obscure eleventh century poet Lin Ho-ching were not surprised. These translations made up the final section of Hanson's first book, *The Distance Anywhere* (University of Washington Press, 1967). In them, Hanson's use of contemporary idiom and reference—"making the scene," "Ed's Happy Haven," "Mt. Pilchuck," for example—may have shaken up the purists among Chinese scholars, but poets were pleased and refreshed. (Indeed, the conservative Chinese scholars who edited *Sunflower Splendor* edited out some of Hanson's elisions and colloquialisms, as one discovers by comparing the versions of Han Yü there with those in Hanson's book, *Growing Old Alive*, Copper Canyon Press, 1979).

"The Divide" is a lovely example of Hanson's method in the earlier book. The essence of it is inimitable, because it relies on a perfect ear. As we all know, poems may be made by fools, but only God can make an ear.

I confess I get moony
when I see these
out of the way places.

Parked for a minute
I look down at
the clapboard houses.

Foot of the hill
I drink spring water
so cold my back teeth ache.

God! Childhood!
how soon I forgot it!

I know of only one other version of this Lin Ho-ching poem in English, by Max Perleberg, which goes as follows: "These villages always
inspire poetic thoughts, / So I alight from my donkey and admire them
for a long time. / At the foot of the frost covered hill I take some water
clear as a mirror. / As I hold it in my mouth, my teeth feel so cold that I
wish to go home." The printer has set this stanza as poetry, but it is all
too evident that it is nothing of the kind.

In the decade or so that Hanson has been translating Han Yü, he has
become more particular in sticking not just to the spirit but to the letter
of the Chinese original; and his colloquialisms are less time-bound,
perhaps as he has realized that some of them, like "making the scene,"
have dated or will date. (However, I assume that Hanson, like Eliot,
believes that every considerable work of literature needs re-translation
every few generations, given the development, distortion and flux of
living languages.)

I don't believe that it is yet sufficiently recognized that much Chinese poetry is, structurally, very loose, by Western standards. Poetry
was a much more casual, even daily, affair than poetry we are accus-
tomed to. This accounts for the vast numbers of poems composed by
the great writers of the Classical period: often four or five thousand
that we know of, and presumably many many more which have been
lost to us. Chinese poetry may be full of afterthoughts, phrases that

Western poets would incorporate, laboriously, into a revision, while his Chinese counterpart has gone blithely on to write 136 more poems: poems as letters to friends; poems as notations of daily observations resembling a diary entry; poems as memorials (in both senses of the term: memoranda and elegy) to high court officials; poems composed for the fun of it at drinking parties, etc. Thus, for a poet who insists that a translation read like an original poem, the work sometimes requires rephrasing or condensation, even the rearrangement of lines to reduce redundancy or anticlimax. (If a translation isn't a poem, "it is like an empty house – where have all the people gone? If it can't read like an original poem, it should read like a blueprint – build it yourself. A blueprint doesn't pretend to be a house that's lived in." – from a letter of Hanson's.)

But more profound than this is the awareness possessed by the handful of great translators from any language: it is necessary to feel your way into the thought processes and emotional responses of the poet you are attempting to translate. In a sense, you become that poet, and he or she becomes you. This cannot take place simply by an act of will or intellect. It can only be described as an intensely *physical* affair. You must perceive language as sound, the sound of meaning. Hanson has said (in another letter) that the Chinese language itself, the ideogram, the calligraphy, forced him to regard a series of sentences as "not like freight-trains, made up of solid static containers hooked together," but as "a sequence of physical activity." He continues: "How mental talk is for most folks! Yet how many intricate stresses, strains, adjustments and struggles of the muscles are involved in even the simplest sound – not to mention a sentence or stanza. To set down a *moving meaning*, to write a poem involving the musculature of utterance is to deal in a way with choreography. . . . " And when you begin to understand the motion, the involuntary gesture, of a poet's thought-language, you are approaching the deepest intimacy with the poet's self.

It should also be remembered that in dealing with poets who wrote a thousand years ago and more, poets like Han Yü and the immortal poets of the T'ang Dynasty, even the most accomplished Chinese scholar – of Chinese birth, I mean – is in effect translating from another language. In addition to changes in a language in a thousand years, characters themselves may have been obscured or obliterated by time. If you have come close to feeling that "sequence of physical activity" in a poet, there is a chance that, given lines a, b and d of a particular stanza, you will be able to reconstruct line c.

It also follows that an accurate academic translation, or prose paraphrase cut up to look like poetry (put together like the "freight-train") may be radically false to the original poem, while a translation which takes certain liberties, recreating the original poem as another poem in English, may also be truer in spirit and feeling to the original. Even Ezra Pound, whose basic understanding of Chinese was so inadequate that he didn't know the proper order of strokes in writing a Chinese character (as is sadly evident in a film made in Pound's last years), was able in "The River Merchant's Wife" to recreate a poem more satisfactorily than the scholarly translations of the time. Now, of course, Pound's influence is so pervasive that many scholars since have been influenced by him — and Hooray for that!

To further clarify these last points, let's compare the only standard translations of Han Yü's "Autumn Thoughts, VII" with Hanson's version. Stephen Owen in *The Poetry of Yeng Chiao and Han Yü*, translates the opening lines as follows:

> Autumn nights never seem to dawn,
> Autumn days darken with terrible ease.
> Since I lack restless, bustling ambition,
> Why do I have sorrow such as this?
> Cold chickens wait in their roosts in vain,
> I'm annoyed so often to see the waning moon. . . .

In *Sunflower Splendor,* Charles Hartman translates the lines thus:

> Autumn nights cannot dawn
> Autumn day turns bitter dark
>
> I have no driving desires
> so why prevails this discontent?
>
> Cold rooster futile on his perch
> the silvered moon I strain to watch. . . .

Mr. Hartman has got rid of those unfortunate cold chickens, reminiscent of Colonel Sanders on a busy night at the drive-in, but I suggest that a phrase like, "so why prevails this discontent?" ("Ah, what prevails the sceptered orb," etc.) has not been speakable in 150 years if, indeed, it ever was. Mr. Owen, though perfectly pedestrian, at least spares us literary inversion. Now Hanson:

> The night is reluctant
> to brighten to dawn
> fall days
>
> grow dark too soon—
> with no driving desires
> why be sad it's autumn?
>
> A shivering rooster
> stuck on his perch
> I peer
>
> at the thin moon. . . .

Note that Hartman makes the comparison between the rooster—or chicken—and the immobile, aging poet implicit, while Hanson completes it. (A good example of how translation, to be really good, requires *decisions*. Try to have it both ways, and you fuzz the poem. Better take a chance of being wrong, and be lucid. Also, Hanson makes clear, as the other two do not, "the dying of the light" in nature and in the man. Stephen Owen gets it right in his notes on the poem although it's missing from his translation: "In the first part of the poem there is an overpowering sense of encroaching darkness, both real and metaphorical. The nights are getting longer with the approach of winter, civilization is also declining."

But to me the chief difference is that one has no particular interest in the Owen or Hartman versions, but one would turn back to Hanson with pleasure, not only because of his elucidation of meaning and implication, but because he is so "anxious to get / the set of the words just right" —to quote from a line of Lin Ho-ching that Hanson once translated with such felicity.

It's also worth noticing that in the first translation the form is conventionally blocky; the lines approach, though clumsily, the standard pentameter line. The second translation is in couplets, and the second inversion of the normal order of syntax occurs because the translator had seen the opportunity for an off-rhyme. Hanson, here and elsewhere, favors a three-line stanza. Why? The use of couplets or four-line stanzas helps contribute to the "freight-train" effect. It becomes fatally easy not to sense the development of one image-thing out of another, and simply to take them one at a time. In *Sunflower Splendor* – this recent and ambitious effort to make the whole sweep of Chinese poetry available to the English reader – the bulk of the translations presents us with lines which, taken one by one, are comprehensible. Each is an autonomous unit, but there is little understanding of the connections, of the flowering of one image from another, of something seen evoking something felt. As the brilliantly articulate inventor of the Moog synthesizer once explained to me, the real problem with *musique concrète* is that when you are purely a technician splicing bits of tape together, it is nearly impossible to *phrase*, to flow. Hanson is a Moog translator, not a note-splicer. The three- or five-line stanza not only tends to be more interesting, now, in English (as the off-rhyme or suppressed rhyme is more interesting than moon-June), but it forces you to redispose the meaning unit so that it flows across the stanzas rather than being wholly contained within the stanza; as with a Moog, one wave (phrase) breaks on the next. You have found a way of showing how one thing grows out of another without having to explain how it happened.

Finally, I want to touch on how and why the translator chooses his poet. Lin Ho-ching and Han Yü have some things in common: neither is in the first rank as to either fame or esteem. Each has been heavily criticized, both by contemporaries and later critics (and Chinese critics have had the curious habit of tending to repeat the criticisms of earlier authorities, unlike the scrutable critics of the West) for roughness, didacticism and for being prosaic. They have been infrequently translated. They both had a considerable contempt for authority, were sometimes stubborn and wrong-headed, and they drank too much. (In these last qualities they were, indeed, not alone among their peers.)

Specifically in regard to Han Yü, you will discover by consulting, say, the *Princeton Encyclopedia of Poetry and Poetics,* that Han Yü has been neglected for a combination of reasons: his main reputation is as a prose writer, rhetorician and philosopher – which obviously complicates any poet's reputation. He wrote a great many discursive and didactic poems. (Hanson has translated only one of these, "The Wild Tiger's Personal Story," because, he explains, they make Han Yü sound like a stuffed shirt. For his two most famous poems, both didactic, "The Stone Drums" and a very long poem about the Southern Mountains, a dazzling linguistic *tour de force,* consult *Sunflower Splendor,* or Owen's book.) Han Yü has been tagged as, philosophically and pragmatically, a Neo-Confucian. You could establish some kind of line of descent here, as Hanson is a Neo-Poundian (his first interest in Chinese poetry came through Pound); and as Pound considers himself a Neo-Neo-Confucian, there you are. But Hanson would say that Han Yü appeals to him because he is a Wyatt, not a Surrey; a Corbière (also thought not to be very "poetic"), not a Laforgue; a Satie, not a Debussy, he is more Browning than Tennyson, and indeed more Pound than Eliot. Hanson has said of him, "I can't think of many poets in any language that I know [and in addition to Chinese, he knows a bit of French, Italian, Provençal – and enough Mongolian to say, "Call off your dogs!"] who even faintly suggest that moral pronouncements are funny." Small wonder, if you are a poet who thoroughly comprehends the nuances of irony, wit and understatement, that you want to use your not inconsiderable skills to translate two poets who were, amid their sadness and self-deprecation, *funny.* Humor – the quality that critics and translators are least capable of understanding or transmitting!

Then too, Hanson's name is not as a poet exactly a household word. But then, in these times, in this place, whose is? Small wonder then to seek out the cranky, the misunderstood, the obscure. The reader could do worse than to try a little Hanson, a little Han Yü.

The Light of Hilda Morley

I HAVE AN AFFINITY for poetry in which the eye and the ear are equal. The ear is primary; it is poetry, after all. We can enjoy, even love or be hypnotized by, poetry which makes melodious noises and little else. There is the overweening music of Swinburne: we know we are not missing anything important as we glide along in his canoe, trailing our fingers in the water and brushing the lily pads. But with Wallace Stevens we may be so bemused by the sounds that we swim over the surface of what he says, and in his case we care about meaning.

Hilda Morley holds with easy aplomb this balance between music and meaning. Our pleasure as readers is physical, almost sensual: "Inside the sea-lily light / stirs / a vibration. / The pulse / of water nourishing the flower . . . "; "I bite down hard on my life . . . "; "the face of the sea astonishing / me forever . . . "; "light-riddled sky-ridden island / like our love / moored to transparencies. . . . "

But I have been diverted from my first point. I refer not so much to mind alone, but to mind's eye. Morley's eye is always seeing, and re-seeing in memory – not just reading or scanning or turning inward on the self. She gives us her pictures, along with a powerful whiff of the other senses: sage on a hot Greek day, wood-smoke when the leaves of fall are burning, odor of earth newly turned by a spade; flavor of cinnamon, heavy silk pouring through the hands, bark of madrona like a Gauguin woman's skin. These sensations are not literally from her poems, but what her poems evoke in one's own breathing imagination.

In reading Morley, as we are wrapped up in seeing, and sensing what we see, we become aware that it is all suffused in light. We are in the presence of the luminosity of memory, and of life remembered, endured, celebrated and transfigured by light. See "That Bright Grey Eye": "The grey sky, lighter & darker / greys, / lights between & deli-

cate / lavenders also... So alight that sky, / late August / early evening... Turner, he should have / seen it, / he would have given it /
back to us, / not let it die away... the sky fiery over the river, / luminous... as Venice seen by Guardi... The pavement / trembles with
light... the light pouring itself away... the light is / without calcula-
tion...." Light is seeing, and sight is light.

In Morley's book, *What Are Winds and What Are Waters* (Matrix
Press), poems to her late husband, the composer Stefan Wolpe, the
first poem says in part:

> "...I see you
> on the porch there in the sunlight,
>   jaunty
> & alert, your legs crossed high,
>   your eyes washed inwardly
> with an extraordinary light,
>   showing
> how filled with it you were,
>   more as if
> light came out of you, than that it came through you,
> that there was a source inside you
> wider & more radiant almost
> than anything you could see
>   Not the sun's light,
> nor the light of many suns,
>   nor the stars could
> give you that illumination...
>   Nature
> which betrayed you brutally
> gave you a light almost beyond itself...."

Light! Light in all its meanings and manifestations. Always the
threnody, the light of the eye – her own, and that of the Beloved. One
wishes one could freshly mint the phrase, "moral radiance" which ema-
nates from the Beloved, and from Hilda Morley herself.

I come late to a thoughtful consideration of Hilda Morley's poetry.
But now she is mine to keep. I say to her as she has said to Sappho: "I
wish never to leave the country of your voice."

An Exaltation of Poets

CAROLYN FORCHÉ

CAROLYN FORCHÉ'S *The Country Between Us* (Harper & Row,
1981) has already won the Lamont Prize, and will win others. Forché
lived for two years in El Salvador, and her courage has been unflinch-
ing, both in her role as endangered witness to horror, and in her com-
mitment to write about it. Once again – and Forché is not alone here –
the poet serves as our conscience. Some with a bad conscience will heap
praise upon her, hoping that there is room for them under her umbrella; some of the rest will take up the stale cry that a true poet does
not concern herself with "politics." These last will go on like this until
they are choked by the first whiff of nerve gas or the first firestorm.
Meanwhile, let me quote Forché back to them:

> Your problem is not your life as it is
> in America, not that your hands, as you
> tell me, are tied to do something. It is
> that you were born to an island of greed
> and grace where you have this sense
> of yourself as apart from others . . .
>
> (from "Return")

> There is a cyclone fence between
> ourselves and the slaughter and behind it
> we hover in a calm protected world like
> netted fish, exactly like netted fish.

It is either the beginning or the end
of the world, and the choice is ourselves
or nothing.

(from "Ourselves or Nothing")

I flinch from quoting terrible and explicit details of blood, torture
and mutilation – "There is nothing one man will not do to another" –
because they are pornographic ripped from the context of Forché's love
and concern for humankind, and of her desperate need to tell us what
we desperately need to hear. But this is the ending of her prose poem,
"The Colonel," which to any of us "with mud on our shoes" – to use a
good phrase of William Atwood's – presents a deadly accurate portrait
of the type of Latino military brute so beloved by a succession of
American administrations to this day:

> The colonel returned with a sack used to bring groceries home.
> He spilled many human ears on the table. They were like dried peach
> halves. There is no other way to say this. He took one of them in his
> hands, shook it in our faces, dropped it into a water glass. It came
> alive there. I am tired of fooling around he said. As for the rights of
> anyone, tell your people they can go f--- themselves. He swept the
> ears to the floor with his arm and held the last of his wine in the air.
> Something for your poetry, no? he said. Some of the ears on the
> floor caught this scrap of his voice. Some of the ears on the floor
> were pressed to the ground.

JOSEPHINE JACOBSEN

JOSEPHINE JACOBSEN'S MIND is exquisite and urbane, which is
not to say that it has confined itself to salon conversation or academic
discourse. In *The Chinese Insomniacs* (University of Pennsylvania Press,
1981) as with her hair-raising stories, *A Walk With Raschid* (Jackpine
Press, 1978), there is a lively sense of the world's evil, told with a
blandness and skill that makes the reader shudder, but never the au-

thor. One could say of all the poets under consideration today (including this reviewer) that, with the exception of Jacobsen, none of us is quite grown up. This means, among other things, that we are not shockproof, that we will always react to fresh horrors as if for the first time. This is to the good, as it annuls world-weariness, leads us to rush at the old targets yet again. Still, how comforting is full maturity!

> The fado singer winged in black
> like The Lodger or a vertical bat,
> black in the green light
> sings of death and love
> of love and treachery, of lonely death and love.
>
> These are conferred on us, trivial
> and happy drinkers, unconsumptive, wed,
> having, all, return tickets to somewhere
> and convivial presumptions. Taller
> we rise as one to agree to his offer.
>
> The fado singer handling our bones and nerves,
> fingers our heart and finds it alive;
> so he tells us we will die, or love will,
> or the one come from the other;
> or we will kill each other, or lose each other . . .
>
> (from "Two Escudos")

Formal and fastidious, Jacobsen meditates on death—oh, not because she herself is aging, nothing even faintly vulgar like that—because of her apprehension of our fleshly frailty. In El Salvador, on her way to the airport, Forché's car rides over a man's intestines, "spread out like a garden hose and I couldn't stop." One feels that somehow Jacobsen has imagined even this:

> I was not there; but have known
> this slaughter, of old.
> I know quite well the night, cold;
> the knife, honed.
>
> (from "The Provider")

There is one further thing about Jacobsen I feel impelled to say, which will do neither her nor me any good with our formidable sisters: she is a lady. The dictionaries are not a lot of help here, because, male-written, they do not mean what I mean, obsessed as they are with rank and status. Piecing bits together from this source and that, I define it thus: she is gentle, tactful and incapable of cruelty, though she under-stands it well. She is the obverse of innocent, and more beautiful.

DENISE LEVERTOV

DENISE LEVERTOV like the late Muriel Rukeyser, is a hero, and indomitable. I see her small, sturdy person, graying now, trudging from reading to meeting, giving her energies without stint to the cause of nuclear disarmament, to justice in Latin America, shrugging off the jeers of the disengaged; yet the hurt is in her eyes, because she is very feminine, vulnerable, human: longing, as we all do, to be cherished, to be cared for. So she is able to seek out and speak to these qualities in others, men as well as women. It is a joy to say that she has worked through the occasional rhetoric and strained proselytizing of *some* of her Vietnam poems (some, of course, are the best of the poems we have of that tortured period, rightfully acknowledged, duly antholo-gized) to the high plateau of this book, *Candles in Babylon* (New Di-rections, 1982) where (to quote her again on the subject of Carolyn Forché's poems) "there is no seam between personal and political, lyri-cal and engaged":

> I send my messages ahead of me.
> You read them, they speak to you
> in siren tongues, ears of flame
> spring from your heads to take them.
>
> When I arrive, you love me,
> for I sing those messages you've
> learned by heart, and bring,
> as housegifts, new ones . . .

But soon you love me less.
I brought with me
too much, too many laden coffers,
the panoply of residence,

improper to a visit.
Silks and furs, my enormous wings,
my crutches, and my spare crutches,
my desire to please, and worse –

my desire to judge what is right...

When I leave, I leave
alone, as I came.

(from "Poet and Person")

In *Light up the Cave* (New Directions, 1981), her interesting collection of essays, Levertov says, "The true heroes and heroines of political radicalism are those who maintain a rich inner life." I would add that a part of that rich life is a saving sense of humor, a delight in play, a self-directed irony – "my crutches, and my spare crutches" – which Josephine Jacobsen knows all about, and a life enriched by reading, myth and dream, as in this by Levertov:

Yes, this year you feel
at a loss, there is no Demeter to whom to return

if for a moment you saw
yourself as Persephone.
It is she, Demeter, has gone
                down to the dark.

Or if it is Orpheus drawing you forth,
Eurydice,
he is inexorable, and does not look back
to let you go...

(from "Talking to Oneself")

The supreme triumph of this book is Levertov's "Mass for the Day of St. Thomas Didymus" (better known as Doubting Thomas), in which she ties together the various threads of her life, from its beginnings—her father was an Anglican clergyman—to the passionate concerns of the present. Here are some fragments from the "Agnus Dei":

> Given that lambs
> are infant sheep, that sheep
> are afraid and foolish, and lack
> the means of self-protection, having
> neither rage nor claws,
> venom nor cunning,
> what then
> is this 'Lamb of God'? . . .
>
> What terror lies concealed
> in strangest words, *O lamb*
> *of God that taketh away*
> *the Sins of the World:* an innocence
>   smelling of ignorance
>   born in bloody snowdrifts,
>   licked by forebearing
> dogs more intelligent than its entire flock put together?
>
>   God then,
>   encompassing all things, is
> defenseless? Omnipotence
> has been tossed away, reduced
> to a wisp of damp wool? . . .
>   . . . is it implied that *we*
> must protect this perversely weak
> animal whose muzzle's nudgings
> suppose there is milk to be found in us?
> Must hold to our icy hearts
> a shivering God? . . .

It is to be hoped that some gifted musician, reading these words, will be impelled to set them to music. Otherwise we may read them aloud to ourselves when we are alone, as my husband did this Easter past, or gather in groups to read them to each other.

From the above, it might seem that the reviewer lacks a certain detachment proper to this enterprise. Let me just clinch it by saying that the next time Denise goes to jail, I plan on going with her.

MARGE PIERCY

MARGE PIERCY IS MY IDEA of the very model of a modern major feminist. There is a deal of sheer, toe-curling pleasure to be gained from reading this robust, protean and hilarious woman's selected poems *Circles on the Water* (Knopf, 1982):

> Athena Pramachos, warrior goddess thirty feet tall,
> no longer exists . . .
> A thousand years she stood over fire and mud,
> then hauled as booty to Constantinople,
> where the Crusaders, bouncy legionnaires
> on the town, melted her down for coins.
>
> These words are pebbles
> sucked from mouth to mouth since Chaucer.
> I don't believe the Etruscans or the Mayans
> lacked poets, only victories.
> Manuscripts under glass, women's quilts packed away
> lie in the attics of museums sealed from the streets
> where the tactical police are clubbing the welfare mothers.
> There are no cameras, so it is not real . . .
>
> (from "Athena in the front lines")

That passage is characteristically funny and acute, but it doesn't display her earthiness, her wonderful *physicalness*. A poem called "Morning athletes," about two women "in mid-lives jogging, awkward / in our baggy improvisations," goes on:

> It is not the running I love, thump
> thump with my leaden feet that only

infrequently are winged and prancing,
but the light that glints off the cattails
as the wind furrows them
. . . the way the pines
blacken the sunlight on their bristles . . .

and your company
as we trot, two friendly dogs leaving
tracks in the sand . . .

In addition to being as fine on the subject of friendship as any T'ang Dynasty Chinese poet, Piercy, who so richly bodies forth the five senses, is wonderful about sex:

Now I look for men whose easy bellies
show a love for the flesh and the table,
men who will come in the kitchen
and sit, who don't think peeling potatoes
makes their penis shrink; men with broad
fingers and purple figgy balls . . .

(from "Cats like angels")

It is good to have the work of seven volumes bound together in one book, along with seven new poems. I miss some old ones, but delight in the discoveries which this kind of gathering reveals. It should be made clear, however, that the passages quoted above do not display Piercy's full range. They could not. This is a woman who can write breathtaking poetry, about making love to a man, and then move into a brilliant diatribe about their inequality ("Doing it differently"):

We will be equal, we say, new man and new woman.
But what man am I equal to before the law of court or custom?
The state owns my womb and hangs a man's name on me
like the tags hung on dogs . . .

Make no mistake. This is a woman totally committed to the freedom of her sex, by any means she can devise, from the blackest and bitterest wit to the sweeping opulence of her very latest work, in which the persona is a woman's version of Mother Courage, as black as Brecht, but as luminous and loving as Marge Piercy:

> Send me your worn hacks of tired themes,
> your dying horses of liberation,
> your poor bony mules of freedom now,
> I am the woman sitting by the river,
> I mend old rebellions and patch them new . . .
>
> I am the old woman sitting by the river scolding corpses.
> I want to stare into the river and see the bottom
> glinting like clean hair,
> I want to outlive my usefulness
> and sing water songs, songs
> in praise of the green brown river
> flowing clean through the blue green world.

(from "Let us gather at the river")

ADRIENNE RICH

PERHAPS ONE REASON WHY so many critics like to concentrate on dead women poets – aside from our growing national necrophilia – is that there will be no surprises. The critic won't have to eat his or her words when the next book comes out. Adrienne Rich is a particularly dangerous proposition in this regard. In recent years, each new book has been a surprise; and a shock to some. Like Levertov, she has a way of working out her preoccupations in public, so that we get the raw as well as the cooked. Sometimes the respectful reader, knowing their track records, makes an unusual effort to empathize, to understand. I confess, then, with some temerity, to having reservations about *A Wild Patience Has Taken Me This Far: Poems 1978–1981* (Norton, 1981). Her wild patience feels more like a cold impatience to me. In her poem, "Rift," Rich says: "Yes, I find you / overweening, obsessed, and even in your genius / narrow-minded," which seems like an apt portrait of the poet herself. When she writes, in "The Images":

> ...when did we ever choose
> to see our bodies strung
> in bondage and crucifixion across the exhausted air
> when did we choose
> to be lynched on the queasy electric signs
> of midtown when did we choose
> to become the masturbator's fix...

I feel that the barricades are up in the war between men and women; the demands are non-negotiable; there will be no compromise, no retreat. And I know that she wants it that way. But to what purpose? It is my hope that one half of the human race is negotiating with the other half, in an attempt to save it. All else is futile crooning over one's wounds as one backs further and further into the cave.

Later in the same poem, Rich goes on:

> I can never romanticize language again
> never deny its power for disguise for mystification
> but the same could be said for music
> or any form created
> painted ceilings beaten gold worm-worn Pietàs
> reorganizing victimization   frescoes translating
> violence into patterns so powerful and pure
> we continually fail to ask are they true for us...

There is a whiff of Calvin or Cromwell in these glittering lines, a whiff of burning tapestry, a thud of statues dashed to the ground, that stirs in me painful echoes of the past, where one set of bigots told the rest of us what we might or might not be permitted to love.

And yet, and yet... The other day, a woman I know who has just undergone a traumatic divorce, told me of her feelings of uncertainty about her son, who seemed to have withdrawn from her during these painful last months. Then, for her birthday, he gave her a copy of *A Wild Patience,* inscribed with these lines from Rich's poem, "Heroines":

> How can I fail to love
> your clarity and fury

> how can I give you
>   all your due
>   take courage from your
>   courage...

Adrienne Rich is used as an instrument of reconciliation, an affirma-
tion of empathy, and by a man too! And so, in Denise Levertov's
words, there is milk to be found in us. Overall, the message of these
splendid women is that we must keep on trying to "hold to our icy
hearts a shivering God."

CAROL MUSKE

THE FIRST POEMS IN Carol Muske's *Wyndmere* (University of
Pittsburgh Press, 1985) are concerned with her mother, a grandmother, a grandfather, in the new light of what it means to her to be a
parent. This is a lighter book than *Skylight* (Doubleday, 1981), her
previous work, not just in its length, but in that it doesn't contain those
glittering arias that made us sit up and take notice. One senses the poet
marking time as she stretches to her full stature. If Miss Muske takes
her time, her next book will show the flowering. This one opens with
"Wyndmere, Windemere" – Wyndmere the place in North Dakota
where her mother was born. "Windemere," meaning "wind-mother," a
lovely conceit, expresses the fragile and volatile nature of this most profound human tie – we know her intimately; we shall never know her.

> The world's wrong, mother,
> Shelley said it when, at the end,
> he got it right. And you, who knew
> every word of his by heart, agreed.
>
> The washed dresses stood on thin air.
> You plucked them with distracted grace,
> a wind-mother...
> *you held me close, you let me go...*
> Poetry's the air we drown in together...

In the wind, on the back step,
I heard the words of poets

who got it right again and again,
in a world so wrong,
it measures only loss
in those crosses of thin air,

in the blowdown and ascent
of the separator, the mother,
whose face catches once,
then turns from me, again and again.

The next poem picks up on the theme of separateness—her grandfather was "a Separator Man, / harvesting the wheat." His threshing machine separated

Strong from weak...
My grandfather died
rich and didn't know it.
No one told him.

By then,
he was too good
at separating—

his wife ten years dead,
his children gone away.
No one to give something to,

no one to witness how
what was taken away
stayed with him—

Next, her grandmother, her brother, a school friend who was raped—handled with a tact that precludes voyeurism, unlike the majority of poems on that anguishing topic. Then Miss Muske dances off into the world of lovers, books, Italy—particularly felicitous, these last—and a fine love poem involving John Tyndall's theory of sight (impurities in the air allow us to see light). She ends with two poems about her daughter. In "August, Los Angeles, Lullaby," as she holds her baby she sees what her mother must have intended for her:

> watching her suck as she
> dreamed of sucking, lightheaded
> with thirst as my blood flowed
>
> suddenly into tissue that
> changed it to milk. No matter
> how close I press, there is a
>
> texture that moves between me
> and whatever might have injured
> us then. Like the curtain's sheer
>
> opacity, it remains drawn
> over what view we have of dawn
> here in this onetime desert,
>
> now green and replenished,
> its perfect climate
> unthreatened in memory—
>
> though outside, as usual,
> the wind blew, the bough bent,
> under the eaves, the hummingbird
>
> touched once the bloodcolored hourglass,
> the feeder, then was gone.

The linkage of blood and blood; the hummingbird, symbol of all that is luminous, swift and ephemeral; the light, sure touch—these are characteristic of Carol Muske's art.

LAURA JENSEN

THERE ARE AT LEAST fifteen poems in *Shelter* (Dragon Gate, 1985), Laura Jensen's third collection, a book of magical spells, that I long to quote in full. The power of originality here is virtually unique in poets of her generation. One springs to attention at lines like these from "Window Views":

> Egret be what we see through,
> the white fog blessedly making
> the ash tree forget its surroundings.
>
> All that is beautiful
> hangs on a thread that is tied to a nail
> in Christ's palm,
> the thread frail as spider web,
> the nail of iron . . .
>
> That is day starting, day says
> hammer, clang at a pipe.
>
> Be there no human here,
> be there here the flat marsh
> before man, be there here
>
> those bony wings,
> arching, convoluting
> powerful illogical opening
> as the white wings
> startle with size at their spread.

Here is a passage from "Dull Brown," a poem with an epigraph – the song title "Easy to Be Hard":

> Easier when a bird flies by
> and flies by smug because
> it builds a nest out of nothing

and builds a shell out of love,
the love that pecks away at hearts
chip, chip, so mindlessly to itself,
the love with its gliding experience.

But when I step out I begin to sob.

Hard to wish
for the wings of an angel, easy
to wish for the wings of a bird
when they are and I am not and it is
so hard to be human, so hard.

Then she can launch a poem with immense authority, like Louise
Bogan at her best, or the noble, neglected Ruth Pitter, as in "Child,":

During the great and humorless invisible winter,
none of the loaves would mold, the air stayed
shiftless, and great dark smears appeared
on the linoleum below the sink, under the witless broom.

And wind it up like this:

During the great uninteresting gray and invisible
winter you forgot about flowers and enough to eat,
about everything but the flat dull house and the
flat dull hours and the invisible landlord's heel.
You forgot the sun, and the renewal of grass.
You forgot friends. Now forget the terrible
unpleasant, unforgivable, humorless invisible winter.
Let it drift out on the air when you open the kitchen
door, just as they say, and hope it goes away.

Other remarkable poems: "Crowsong," "Earlier," "I'll Make You a
Cat," "Butterflies," "Calling," "I Want to Walk Out." Sometimes Miss
Jensen sings purely to herself; we overhear the words, some muffled.
We hear sharp little cries of pain. But there is a calm, almost a placidity
at her center, sometimes a mad calm. Once in a while she has trouble
with closure. The last stanza will drift off as if her attention had been

caught by something gleaming, arcane. This is what comes of her free, darting imagination, like – yes – a hummingbird. Like a bowerbird. Like a poet.

JOHN ASH

IT IS STARTLING, and a little touching for a poet of my generation (oldish), to see the ghosts of Eliot and Auden stalking the psyche of John Ash in *The Branching Stairs* (Carcanet, 1984). Some of *their* antecedents – Proust, Baudelaire, Laforgue – hover as well, as in these examples:

> we suddenly remember the one
> who died in Canada towards the end of winter. . . .
> The spectacle is over for us
> (the hotel and the casino fall back into ruin)
> we are outside and a morning
> that is infinitely unsure of itself
> begins to take shape over the harbour
>
> The cafes are closing as they will always close
> And our glasses are once more empty –
>
>   Then accompanied
> by a brief exhalation of stale harmonies a crowd
> pressed onto the terrace of the casino
> to watch the departure that was taking place
>
> under a cloud formation like a suspended lamp
> of red faceted glass (and we –
> all of us! recalled our first visit to the theatre)
>
> Vittorio is dining with
> that Chinese actress again . . .
> Will the kingdom be divided?
> Who will keep
> the chandeliers in good repair

and tend the lists of public enemies? . . .
O, O, O, O . . .

O, O, O, O, the poet knows himself best: "You can almost smell the
lavender water / The word 'Proustian' comes to mind." The word "brilliant" also comes to mind. Once these lavender excursions are con-
cluded, Mr. Ash moves with brisk authority to "Even Though":

> the suspension bridges are buckling in the hurricane
> and several cars full of conventional families
> with an average number of children have been thrown
> into a river full of alligators.

Which ends: "We have stepped into the frontispiece of a new book: / it
is called *The History of Pleasure*."

Here are passages from "Bespalko's Devotions":

> The summer trees are dark where the yellow oriole sings.
> Exiles are writing their sonnets to autumn.
>
> Walking back from the post office,
> clutching parcels of censored mail
> they glance uneasily at the sky. . . .
>
> They drink and they talk and they count —
> hours, days, miles and seasons. They fear
> the rigours of our winters, the wide streets frozen
> and open to the winds, the walls leaking cold. . . .
>
> In the night they press their ears
> to ancient radios only to hear
> themselves or their friends condemned.
>
> They fear the time when they cease to recognize
> the names in the anathemas.

There is more, much more. This is a substantial volume. Now if Mr.
Ash will quit posturing and calm down. A little querulous, perhaps?
Never mind. This may be the most auspicious debut of its kind since
Auden's.

LORINE NIEDECKER

IN READING Lorine Niedecker, one feels that if one had grown up on a desert island, or in an American small town (much the same thing), one could have learned how to be a poet from Lorine Niedecker. Her own world, indeed, was a severely circumscribed one. She lived her life on Black Hawk Island, near where she had been born, on the edge of Lake Koshkonong in Wisconsin.

> My life
>   by water—
>   Hear
>
> spring's
>   first frog
>   or board
>
> out on the cold
>   ground
>   giving
>
> Muskrats
>   gnawing
>   doors
>
> to wild-green
>   arts and letters
>   Rabbits
>
> raided
>   my lettuce
>   One boat
>
> two—
>   pointed toward
>   my shore

> thru birdstart
> wingdrip
> weed-drift

> of the soft
> and serious —
> Water

One's first impulse, after awe, on reading *The Granite Pail* (North Point Press, 1985) is a double dose of shame: shame at not being more familiar with her work; shame at ever having complained of the narrowness of one's life — not enough parties, not enough flattery, not enough interesting intellectual friends. She is exemplary in the way that Dickinson is, or Mary Barnard. She makes you resolve, through tears, to clean up your act. Why go on and on about oneself, as so many of us do, when you can describe a whole life in a handful of lines? — as in a little poem about finding a green tree toad and saying, "Let's take it in / I said so grandmother can see / but she could not / it changed to brown / and town / changed us, too."

Or the second stanza about her mother, dying:

> "It's a long day since last night.
> Give me space. I need
> floors. Wash the floors, Lorine! —
> wash clothes! Weed!"

We think of Dr. Williams. We think of St. Francis — "My friend tree / I sawed you down . . ." We think of the finest Japanese *and* Chinese poetry — "We said good-bye / on The Passing Years / River"; or

> Swept snow, Li Po,
> by dawn's 40-watt moon
> to the road that hies to office
> away from home.

> Tended my brown little stove
> as one would a cow — she gives heat.
> Spring — marsh frog-clatter peace
> breaks out.

We think of writing Lorine Niedecker a letter. But she has been dead since 1970. So we think of sending this book to our seven best friends.

EDWARD HIRSCH

No ONE COULD SAY that Edward Hirsch isn't daring or eccentric, thank goodness. Yet I sensed two things in *Wild Gratitude* (Knopf, 1986): first, that his eccentricities may be veering close to becoming mannerisms, and second, *now* I think I see what some very young poets are imitating – as in the following passage from "Sleepwatch":

> ... But, inside, a moon shivers in the spaces
> between your wife's outstretched arms, between
> her shoulders and her legs, between the skin

> of water pulled over her watery lungs
> and the white egg growing
> larger and larger in her chest. This is
> the same moon that shudders in darkness
> inside of darkness, behind your eyes.

Miss Niedecker would probably not approve, and I'm not sure I do, but it certainly doesn't stink of Iowa City. Hirsch is also capable of committing the following:

> But nothing helped. When my mother finally died
> I dreamt the full moon was a tumor of the uterus,
> My body was pressed under the purple iron of night.

However, Hirsch's great strength lies in his descriptive powers, as in these final stanzas of his poem about Edward Hopper (by the way, what is this Hopper cult among the young? I have at least three new books with Hoppers on the cover, and *homages* as common as *fromages*):

And then one day the man simply disappears.
He is a last afternoon shadow moving
Across the tracks, making its way
Through the vast, darkening fields.

This man will paint other abandoned mansions,
And faded cafeteria windows, and poorly lettered
Storefronts on the edges of small towns.
Always they will have this same expression,

The utterly naked look of someone
Being stared at, someone American and gawky,
Someone who is about to be left alone
Again, and can no longer stand it.

That is so loving, and so exact, that some painter who had never seen a Hopper might be able to produce a reasonable facsimile from the description. And it catches the lonely, ascetic spirit of Hopper in a way that moves you as the painting moves you.

There is another fine poem about a village idiot, who "could also sit on the hillside for days / like a dim-witted pelican staring at the fish." So, as we see, there is a nice movement in his work from the almost ridiculous to the nearly sublime. One puts down the book smiling, wishing him luck.

LINDA GREGG

LINDA GREGG is a brilliant flawed poet; brilliant in her detachment when she is watchful, lost in what she sees, nursing her own insights, lost in her songs; flawed when autobiographical detail is so intimate that you blush for her:

It has been a long time now
since I stood in our dark room looking
across the court at my husband in her apartment.
Watched them make love . . .

Or this, the beginning of "Something Scary" from *Alma* (Random House, 1985):

> Over the phone Joel tells me
> his marriage is suddenly miraculous.
> That his wife is glad now about us.
> Is even grateful.
> "We have crossed a border," he says.
> I listen, knowing myself too far gone
> to last more than a day.

The flaws, one feels, are due to what might be called a continuing crisis of confidence: as if she felt that to be *real* she had to tell us things about herself we don't need to know, as if her readers were a mirror into which she gazes with an almost pitiable uncertainty, to assure herself that she is present.

Unfortunately, we live in a society which cheers at naked self-exposure, and cares little if the stripper burns or freezes. But I care, as all people who love poetry for itself, poetry transcending personality, care. We long to say, "You're glorious. You're remarkable. Now *move on out!*" Listen to her when she does:

> Far is where I am near.
> Far is where I live.
> My house is in the far.
> The night is still.
> A dog barks from a farm.
> A tiny dog not far below.
> The bark is soft and small.
> A lamp keeps the stars away.
> If I go out there they are.

A lovely ambiguity in that last line – so different from "knowing myself too far gone . . ." A faint echo of Roethke – and why not?

Or say aloud this lovely thing, "Trying to Believe": personal, yes, but meta-personal, as in *metaphysical:*

>There's nothing gentle where Aphrodite was.
>Empty mountain and grasshoppers banging
>into me. Maybe there never was.
>But I go up again and again to search
>under thorn bushes and rocks.
>Am grateful for the marble arm
>big as my thumb. A shard with a man's feet
>and a shard with the feet of a bird. A sign
>that it can be more. Like when a wind comes
>in the great heat and lifts at my body.
>Like when I get back to my mountain, aching
>and my hands hurt. Sit alone looking down at
>evening on the ocean, drinking wine or not.

Aroma of Greece, of Seferis: "haunted Seferis, playing with his beads," in the wonderful phrase of Bernard Spencer. "All Greece goes through me . . ." Yes.

There are a dozen poems of this quality in *Alma* which make it worth your attention. And hope for her growth, her healing, her long, confident stride towards becoming a major poet.

C.K. WILLIAMS

To me, C.K. Williams is the most exciting poet writing today. In *Tar* (Random House, 1983) one's fascination is divided between the extraordinarily long, flexible lines extending from margin to margin—like those of no other poet now writing—lines that may seem prosy on first reading, but are not—and his subject matter. Nothing more remote from academic writing could be imagined. The scenes: working-class bars, substandard houses, soiled city streets, gas stations, abandoned mines. Real places. The characters: a paraplegic Vietnam vet, a middle-aged woman walking her sick dog, a sixty-year-old gambler, an old-age pensioner, a drunken woman screaming in the night. Real people and real suffering—and honest perceptions and empathies painfully arrived at.

To my knowledge, other than Williams, only Philip Levine and Gerald Stern deal with the ordinary lives of Americans who haven't been to college, but not as consistently, though I admire them too. It's not that they have never dwelt in academe or taught in poetry workshops. They have. But the pervasive blight of writing a poem in order to have written a poem – or worse, in order to get it into print as rapidly as possible – has not affected these men.

Space prevents me from quoting nearly as much Williams as I would like. But let me describe and quote from a single poem. "Combat" (whose characters are not typical of him, but whose method is): The poet sees a welterweight fighter on TV who reminds him of "a girl I knew once, a woman . . . the same rigorous carriage same facial structure – sharp cheekbones . . . even the sheen of perspiration." She and her mother were aristocractic German refugees: "their apartment was, in fact, the most splendid thing I'd ever seen." Moira's father had been a general involved in the conspiracy against Hitler, and had killed himself when the plot failed. Moira told him this story over and over: the father's suicide, the mother and child's escape, the awful details while the poet was attempting to make love to her, "with such compassion, such generous concern, such cunning twenty-one-year-old commiseration." "We'd touch that way – petting was the word then – like lovers, with the mother right there with us." There seemed something, "some complicity between them, some very adult undertaking / that I sensed but couldn't understand . . . "

"Later, when I was studying the Holocaust, I found it again, the name, Von C. . . . , in Shirer's *Reich:* / it had indeed existed, and it had, yes, somewhere on the Eastern front, blown its noble head off. / I wasn't very moved. I wasn't in that city anymore . . . and besides, I'd changed by then – I was more aware of history and was beginning to realize, / however tardily, that one's moral structures tended to be air unless you grounded them in real events . . . "

But why had these strenuous sexual struggles, "mauling each other like demented athletes," gone on for so long? the poet muses. "What am I doing in that room, a tea-cup trembling on my knee, that odd, barbed name mangled in my mouth?" "I wonder, putting it most simply, leaving out humiliation, anything like that, if I might have been their Jew? / I wonder. I mean, if I might have been an implement for them, not of atonement – I would have nosed that out – / but of absolution, what they'd have used to get them shed of something rankling – history, it would be . . . that part of it at least / which so befouled the rest . . ." And, at the end: "Beautiful memory, most precious and most treacherous sister: what temples must we build for you. / And even then, how belatedly you open to us; even then, with what exuberance you cross us."

Even with the drastic cuts I've made, you see the splendor of his syntax; you sense the honesty, tenderness and complexity of that mind. You hear an authentically new voice in American poetry, a voice which couldn't be anything *but* American. That is part of its glory, and a triumphant refutation of those who sourly tell us that our poetry today is a poor thing.

FRANK BIDART

Having said Williams is exciting, I must now say that Bidart is mesmerizing – equally original, and, like Williams, basically a narrative poet. Random House enclosed an interview with Bidart along with their review copy of *The Sacrifice* (Random House, 1983), which goes a long way towards explaining his methods. Excerpts: "The heart of my first book was . . . autobiographical; but how I came to this subject matter is bound up with discovering a prosody, figuring out how to write down, how to 'fasten to the page' the voice – and the movements of the voice – in my head." He goes on to say that, as a young writer, you turn from literature, particularly the modernists, and look at your own life, "NOTHING is figured out; NOTHING is understood. EVERYTHING remains to be done." (Upper case Bidart's.) So he uses punctuation and upper case to articulate the movement of the voice in his head, "express the relative weight and importance of the parts of the sentence." "This allows me to lay out the bones of a sentence visually, spatially, so that the reader can see the pauses, emphases, urgencies and languors in the voice."

When Bidart discusses his poem about Nijinsky—the heart of this new book, a poem of thirty-two pages—he says. "The Nijinsky poem was a nightmare...Nijinsky's ferocity, the extent to which his mind is radical, scared me...the movement of his voice is so mercurial and paradoxical: many simple declarative sentences, then a long, self-loathing, twisted-against-itself sentence. The volume of the voice (from very quiet to extremely loud) was new: I found that many words and phrases had to be not only entirely capitalized, but in italics."

I have quoted from the interview so extensively for two reasons: first, because Bidart's ordinary speaking voice is extraordinarily similar to his poetic one; second, because I wouldn't want you to be put off by the use of italics and upper case in the poems, which, at first glance, might seem to be SHOUTING. Really it is an addition to the musical notation of poetry. Now, a few passages from "The War of Vaslav Nijinsky":

> —Last night, once again, I nearly
> abandoned my autobiographical ballet...
>
> The plot has a good beginning
> and middle,—
>   THE PUZZLE
>
> is the end...
>
> The nights I spend—
>
>   reading and improving
> Nietzsche, analysing and then abandoning
> my life, working on the *Great Questions*
>
> like WAR and GUILT and GOD
> and MADNESS,—
>
> rise from my books, my endless, fascinating
> researches, notations, projects,
>
> dazzled.
>   —Is this happiness?...

And this passage, almost at the end of the poem:

> *I must chop down the Tree of Life*
> *to make coffins . . .*
>
> Tomorrow I will go to Zurich –
> to live in an asylum.
>
> MY SOUL IS SICK, –
>   NOT MY MIND.
>
> I *am* incurable . . . I did not
> live long.
>
> Death came
> unexpectedly, –
>   *for I wanted it to come.*
>
> Romola. Diaghilev.
>
> . . . I HAVE EATEN THE WORLD
>
> *My life is the expiation for my life.*

Nijinsky was a great physical genius – and so is the poet who has written in his voice. Poetry *physical?* Believe it. As Bidart remarked the other day, we type the pages over and over, until we get them into our muscles. There is no way to solve a poem except by making it a part of your body. We perceive language as sound: the sound of meaning. That is one reasons why poets will be among the last holdouts in a computerized world.

ROBERT HASS

ROBERT HASS IS SO intelligent that to read his poetry or prose, or to hear him speak gives one an almost visceral pleasure. He is the master of what I have named the reticule poem. A reticule, friends, is a capacious bag carried by some of our grandmothers, which might contain her knitting, cough drops, gloves, a tin of cookies, a volume of Wordsworth or Jane Austen or a missal; her coin purse, shopping list, makeup, and a little folder of family snapshots. In short, her necessities of life. That would have been a good title for Hass if it hadn't been used by Adrienne Rich.

One can say that all these disparate articles go together because they *are* together, in one bag. But it is his associative processes, his associated sounds, and his strategies which enhance, combine and weave together these elements which give his poems their rich and singular flavor. Some lines from "Santa Barbara Road" from *Human Wishes* (Ecco Press, 1989):

> . . . when Luke was four or five
> he would go out . . . and still in his dandelion-
> yellow pajamas on May mornings
> and lie down on the first warm stone . . .

> . . . one April, walking into the kitchen,
> I felt like a stranger to my life . . .

> . . . Later, on street corners,
> you can hardly see the children, chirping
> and shivering, each shrill voice climbing over
> the next . . . "Wait, you guys,"
> one little girl says, trying to be heard.
> "Wait, wait, wait, wait, wait."

> . . . Richard, who had recently divorced,
> idly rolling a ball with someone else's child,
> healing slowly, as the neighbor's silky mare
> who had had a hard birth in the early spring,
> stood quiet in the field as May grew sweet,
> her torn vagina healing. So many visions
> intersecting at what we call the crystal
> of a common world . . .

> . . . Leif comes home from the last day of his sophomore year.
> I am sitting on the stoop by our half-dug,

> Still-imagined kitchen porch, reading
> Han Dynasty rhyme-prose. He puts a hand on my shoulder,
> grown exactly my height and still growing.
> "Dad," he says, "I'm not taking any more
> of this tyrannical bullshit." I read to him
> from Chia Ya: *The great man is without bent,*
> *a million changes are as one to him.*
> He says, "And another thing, don't lay
> your Buddhist trips on me." *The span of life is fated;*
> *man cannot guess its ending . . .*

Like the poems of his contemporaries, C. K. Williams and Frank Bidart, these poems need to be heard, be spoken: resonances, pauses, intonations, the vocal music. But unlike them, Hass is a poet of domestic passion – for children, for friends, for the household, the neighborhood, women as lovers, women as friends. The publisher's letter which accompanies this book speaks of his work as poems of loss, of mutilation. Rather, he is a poet of abundance, a romantic of the breakfast table, of a companionable walk in the California hills. Perhaps his publisher was bemused – as well she might have been – by Hass's elegy to a vanished life, a miscarried child, called "Thin Air." This noble poem which defies paraphrase and should not be amputated by quotation is the keystone of a remarkable book.

JAMES MERRILL

THINK OF THE pleasure and pain that James Merrill has given us over the years, we readers and writers, the pleasure of great music superbly performed, the pain amounting to despair of fellow poets as they have contemplated his unattainable perfection. I look at my bookshelf which contains a procession of ambient *M*'s: Meredith, Merrill, Merwin. All of their books are present except for Merrill's *First Poems* (Knopf, 1951), which someone has pinched. Old favorites speak to me: the Europa sonnet in couplets from his second book which ends,

> . . . Who comes to pray remains to scoff
> At tattered bulls on shut church doors
> In black towns numberless as pores,
> The god at last indifferent
> And she no longer chaste but continent.

Rich with parody and pun! – particularly the last outrageous word. I remember "After Greece" from his next book, with its unforgettable opening:

> Light into the olive entered
> And was oil. Rain made the huge pale stones
> Shine from within . . .

And from *The Firescreen* (Atheneum, 1969), my favorite poem, and his: "Matinees," where eight sonnets are strung together followed by eight short stanzas, on a boy's first visit to the opera, in Mrs. Livingston's box: " . . . with pulsing wealth the house is filled, / No one believing, everybody thrilled . . . " There follows "the household opera" of the boy becoming the poet:

> . . . Flesh knows by now what dishes to avoid,
> Tries not to brood on bomb or heart attack.
> Anatomy is destiny, said Freud.
> Soul is the brilliant hypochondriac.
> Soul will cough blood and sing, and softer sing . . .

One has to stop and laugh in memory of that impudent send-up of Yeats. The poem continues:

> . . . What havoc certain Saturday afternoons
> Wrought upon a bright young person's morals
> I now leave to the public to condemn.

> The point thereafter was to arrange for one's
> Own chills and fever, passions and betrayals,
> Chiefly in order to make a song of them . . .

Then with a wonderful turning at the conclusion Merrill, again the little boy, composes his thank-you note:

> . . . Dear Mrs. Livingston,
> I want to say that I am still in a daze
> From yesterday afternoon.
> I will treasure the experience always . . .

And I will too. Presently, with this volume, I am adding some new treasures. I'm there, with him in *The Inner Room* (Alfred A. Knopf, 1988), listening to Merrill's musical offering, wry, plangent, still remorse-lessly punning, though puns such as "disposable issues and cleansing screams" may seem a little tired.

Thanks to a trip to Japan, he is trying something new – a combination of poetry and prose. (*His* jacket copy compares him to Bashō, nor need he be. He's Merrill.) In "Afternoons at the Noh," a detailed prose passage ends:

> The eight-pawn chorus is chanting in antiphon with
> Tsunemasa – a droning, fluctuating,
>   slowly-swelling hymn:
>   the god's fingertip circling
>   one deep vessel's rim
> after another, until all the voices are attuned.

The last poem in this series, called, "In the Shop," speaks of a "fabulous kimono" of crêpe de Chine, and meditates on the homophone of dyeing with dying. A shadow has fallen across this book, the terrible shadow of AIDS. Almost the last poems in this book are dedicated to David Kalstone, poems which also appear in the extraordinary anthology, *Poets for Life, 76 poets respond to AIDS* (Crown, 1989). In "Final Performance, the poet scatters the ashes of his friend in the water,

> (Past) sunny, fluent soundings that gruel of selfhood
> taking manlike shape for one last jeté on
> ghostly – wait, ah! – point into darkness vanished.
> High up, a gull's wings

clapped. The house lights (always supposing, caro,
Earth remains your house) at their brightest set the
scene for good: true colors, the sun-warm hand to
cover my wet one . . .

With that Hopkins-like gasp – wait, ah! – the poem trembles towards
its conclusion, another scene in the opera of Merrill's life.

Finally it occurs to me, with a slap of the forehead for being so ob-
tuse, that Merrill is a great love poet. There have been so many breathtaking feats of prestidigitation before our busy eyes that this may have
escaped our notice. But it's true. Most of his poems breathe with love.
And that is another, and even greater gift that he has given us.

DAN PAGIS

I MET DAN PAGIS just once, nearly twenty years ago, at a poetry
festival in Belgium. We stayed up most of the night with two other
Israeli poets and talked and talked. What talk! I thought him the most
incandescently intelligent person I had ever met. I cherished the memory of that evening, and when I heard of his death three years ago I
mourned him as if he had been my friend, my brother, with whom I
had been in touch ever since. So when his book of his poems, *Variable
Directions* (North Point, 1989) came into my hands, it was as if he
had been restored to me. I want to quote a poem of his, complete, so
that you too may come to know this rare being. It is called "Autobiography":

> I died with the first blow and was buried
> among the rocks of the field.
> The raven taught my parents
> what to do with me.
>
> If my family is famous,
> not a little of the credit goes to me.
> My brother invented murder,

my parents invented grief,
I invented silence.
Afterwards the well-known events took place.
Our inventions were perfected. One thing led to another,
orders were given. There were those who murdered in their
      own way,
grieved in their own way.

I won't mention names
out of consideration for the reader,
since at first the details horrify
though finally they're a bore:

you can die once, twice, even seven times,
but you can't die a thousand times.
I can.
My underground cells reach everywhere.

When Cain began to multiply on the face of the earth,
I began to multiply in the belly of the earth,
and my strength has long been greater than his.
His legions desert him and go over to me,
and even this is only half a revenge.

    Dan Pagis was born in 1930 in Bukovina, once a part of Austria, then Romania, now the Soviet Union. He spent three years in a concentration camp. In 1946 he emigrated to Israel, learned Hebrew, and eventually became a professor of medieval Hebrew literature. He was in his mid-fifties when he died of cancer. Tormented by his memories, then tormented by terrible pain when relief was denied him on the grounds that his ailment was psychomatic, he found serenity in the last months of his life, so a friend tells me. Reader, remember him.